SHE SAY,
HE SAY

She Say, He Say

Urban Girls Write Their Lives

Brett Elizabeth Blake

STATE UNIVERSITY OF NEW YORK PRESS

Published by
State University of New York Press, Albany

For information, address State University of New York
Press, State University Plaza, Albany, N.Y., 12246

Production by Diane Ganeles
Marketing by Fran Keneston

Library of Congress Cataloging-in-Publication Data

Blake, Brett Elizabeth.
    She say, he say : urban girls write their lives / by Brett
Elizabeth Blake.
        p.   cm.
    Includes bibliographical references and index.
    ISBN 0-7914-3479-6 (hc : alk. paper). — ISBN 0-7914-3480-X (pb :
alk. paper)
    1. English language—Composition and exercises—Study and teaching
(Elementary)—United States—Case studies. 2. Women—Education
(Elementary)—United States—Case studies. 3. Education, Urban-
-United States—Case studies. 4. Socially handicapped children-
-Education (Elementary)—United States—Case studies. 5. Critical
pedagogy—United States—Case studies. I. Title.
LB1576B496 1997
372.62'3—dc21   96-45352
                                                              CIP

10   9   8   7   6   5   4   3   2   1

To Robbie

*May your voice resound clearly,
confidently, honestly, and
passionately as you grow with this world.*

Contents

Foreword

Here is Teresa's hope:

> When I grow up I want to achieve a career as a nurse. I want to be a nurse because I would help sick people. When you get your first pay check, you could buy a house if you save your money I would save a lot of money so I could get a car. I would take my family. I will support to have 2 kid and good husband. I will send my mother money or rent and other stuff. If my mother don't have a car I will give her a ride when she don't know how to drive. My family would live happily [ever after].

Her close friend Alejandra provides variations on the theme:

> When I grow up I want to be a Nurse so I could help them feel better. I like to be a nurse because you could give shots to people. In the hospital you have stay up and you don't get no sleep. In the hospital you have to write a lot of stuff to give to the paingent [patient]. I like when we take a break and do all you want. In the hospital sometime the Nurse get of woke [gets awakened]. I want to be a nurse because I to a wondful like [I too want a wonderful life].

And Chantal's modest dream is not far away:

> When I grow up I will finish school. I will work at McDonalds. When I get my pay check I will by me a

house. before I get marry. I will buy a car and I will be driving it all day long. Then I will get marry and go on a honeymoon. Then I will have a baby. Her name will be Alexzandra. My husband will be working until my baby be going to school Then I be working at McDonalds.

Teresa, Alejandra, and Chantal are three of the city kids you will meet through the steady work and interpretive eye of Brett Blake. Mostly Latinas and immigrant and bilingual, mostly ten-years-old, all poor, the girls of the Writer's Workshop assemble regularly to gossip, to tease, to rehearse their impending adolescence, to confess, to share feelings and fantasies and fears. Most important the girls assemble to write, and they discover in the Writers Workshop a public space with explicit permission to narrate, with official sanction to take off. And they do take off, creating a blizzard of words, writing their lives, raising their voices, telling their tales. The proliferating themes are their own: Boys We Hate, What's Unfair, Babies Who Have Babies, Periods. Their writing—like their lives—is unfinished and incomplete, of course, but it is also full of energy and immediacy and drive—it opens opportunities for each young woman to pause and wonder about who she is, where she's been, and where she's heading. Editing text becomes a powerful lesson and metaphor for editing experience. As the participants begin to see themselves as the major actors and stars in their own stories, writing becomes linked to choice and action, intentionality and agency in their own lives. A story is crafted; a life is storied. The teacher's message is this: you can write your story, and you can also author your life.

Laurelei writes of a fantasy slumber party:

Once there was a girl named Judie . . . One day she decided that she was going to make a slumber party at her house and that it was going to be fun. She decided She was going to invite all her friends from school, except the boys, of course! It was going to be a girls slumber party . . . So, that Friday night, all her friends came . . . I don't Know how, but one of the boys Knew that we were having a slumber party, so that boy told the other boy's and they decided they were going to pick on us. It was so embarrassing. They brought a ladder and climbed at my bedroom window. We were playing like we were movie stars. So we were moving like we were big and we were dancing and waling and acting up. When I turned around, I saw a boy at my bedroom window and I started yelling. Then all the girls Went to the bedroom window and started hitting the boys in the head with the pillows . . . all of a studden, the ladder came down and the boys went "Wooaaa!" . . .

After the boys are grounded by their angry mothers, the narrator tells each boy, "I am having another slumber party. Wanna come?"

Nayda invents a scene to account for an unimaginable loss:

When I was 4 years old my Dad, Nick took me to Indiana for the first time. I asked my Mom if she wanted to go she said, "No." So, I went to Indiana. Then my Dad took me to a store called Frank's and I got lost. Then I couldn't find my Dad. I went around the whole store and I found my Dad . . . So my Dad took me in the car and he went back in the store to finish buying what he had to buy . . . I was messing with the shifting gear and when I stopped playing with the gear, I noticed that the car was moving. Then I jumped out of the car and I broke my ankle. The car kept on moving and it crashed into the store. Then it blew up and all the people from the store ran out. When my Dad Nick came out, he was mad. His face was cherry red, his eyes looked like they were going to pop out. I was going to run, but I couldn't beacause I broke my ankle . . . My dad took me to my house and my mom, Carin, saw the cast and started fighting with my Dad. My mom threw my dad out of the house and I never saw my dad ever again.

* * *

The language of these writers if full of zip and vigor:

The sun is a star . . . The sun's energy lifts the water out of the oceans and makes the rain. The sun's energy makes hurricanes and rainbows . . . The sun may be just a star in the universe but in the Solar System it's giant . . . Alejandra

Never kiss an alligator, hug, an alligator, pat, poke, push, hit, kick or even touch an alligator, because alligators bite! . . . The name alligator is from a Spanish world "el lagarto" which means the lizard. Lizards do look like miniature alligators . . . Maribel

Language, of course, is how any of us meets the world, how we greet one another, how we make sense of who we are. Travelling in the Arab world with Palestinian friends recently I was struck by how much one's understanding of life is carried in the language—the constant references to Allah's will, for example, in accepting one's lot; the piling on of honorifics and the escalating granting of titles in ordinary conversation. Although we are largely unaware of it in our daily life—language is as invisible as the air we breathe—language is who we are. Words are us.

Good teachers understand this: they embrace students as they are, honor the dreams and aspirations they bring with them to school, assume an intelligence and capacity that may not be visible but is certaintly present, fortify them to name themselves with courage and hope. Good teachers see their students as three-dimensional beings, hear their voices as nuanced and dynamic, grounded and acute.

But there is more: good teachers challenge students as well, they build bridges from the known to the outer boundaries and the not-yet-known. Good teachers don't merely hear their students; good teachers talk back.

* * *

As these youngsters—multiply-marginalized in a society that despises the poor, creates walls of exclusion for non-English speaking immigrants and people of color, and privileges men—write their lives, we see, finally, the reason to teach and the reason to inquire into the lifeworld of the

Writer's Workshop: it is a humanizing project. Becoming attuned to the voices of these students is to allow them in a real sense to become the teachers of their teachers. They are—if we will allow it—not only stars in their own stories but small heroes in our worlds as well.

This work, then, is undertaken with faith—faith in the mysterious depth and infinite complexity of life as it is lived, commitment to an enduring expectation that people can be better. It is tempered by the certainty that every attempt to convey a life is partial and contingent. It may extend the natural history of children in schools, it may enlarge our understandings of choice and language and writing, but it is not the last word. It may be an important antidote to authoritarian research and empty promises. It can contribute more details, more instances, more cases. Still, there is always more to say. This is one utterance. Read. Talk back.

WILLIAM AYERS

Professor of Education
University of Illinois at Chicago

Acknowledgments

This book would not be complete if I did not thank the many people in my life who have supported and encouraged my work. In the words of Emerson, these family members, friends, and colleagues helped me to not only laugh often, but to breathe a little easier.

First, I would like to thank my dissertation committee and former professors, Chris Pappas, Victoria Chou, Sabrina Hope King, Rae Moses, and Bill Schubert for their insistence that I revise my dissertation study into a book. Collectively, their insight into the value of qualitative inquiry, narrative, and the varied contexts of urban public education has continued to greatly influence my own senses of what is worthwhile to know and experience. A special thanks to Bill Ayers who not only taught me that to learn to write, one had to write, but also who (along with Leigh O'Brien and Mara Sapon-Shevin over lunch) helped with the book title in thought-provoking, yet un-thought of ways!

Second, I would like to thank my family, who without doubt has helped me to breathe a little easier. My father, as my mentor, has given me unwavering support along with stories and resources collected over 40 years in the field. His continued faith in not only the potential of "education," but also in the potential of "educators" remains a powerful inspiration for me to continue my work, even in the most frustrating of circumstances. Thanks also to my mother for helping me in my other profession—parenthood, my brother David for showing me what true courage is, my brother Bob for continuing to be my very dear confidant, and my grandmother, Grace, who reminds me in very subtle ways what "grace" is and how one lives it.

A warm thank you to all my friends and colleagues, who are the definitive source of my being able to laugh often—Maureen Daw, Beth Dohrn, John Lee, Marge Mulhern, April Naumann, and Celia Oyler as fellow graduate students, Kate Daboll-Lavoie, Joyce Dickinson-Mackin, Deb First, Tim Glander, Alice Jones, Esther Maltese, Leigh O'Brien, and Ken Weiss as colleagues at Nazareth College, Stephanie Kuhn and Colleen Lonigan as my graduate assistants—Colleen's insight and hard work on editing and indexing has only made this work richer—Frank Benchik, Betsy Bohmer, Laura Leeper, Judi Lester, Linda Pickering, and Anne-Pat Wurtenberg for remaining good friends throughout various stages of my life and work, and to "Bud" whose wet kisses and unconditional love helped me to remember that we are not always the center of the universe.

And finally, thank you to Mr. Roscoe, whose tenacity and commitment, through his daily challenges, inspired me to listen to the eleven girls whom he taught. Their voices have changed my life forever.

1

Introduction

What we had not anticipated was that "voice" was more than academic shorthand for a person's point of view. We became aware that it is a metaphor that can apply to many aspects of women's experience and development. In describing their lives, women commonly talked about voice and silence: "speaking up," "speaking out," "being silenced," "not being heard," and so on in an endless variety of connotations all having to do with a sense of mind, self-worth, and feelings of isolation from or connection to others. We found that women repeatedly used the metaphor of voice to depict their intellectual and ethical development; and that the development of a sense of voice, mind, and self, were intricately intertwined. (Belenky, Clinchy, Goldberger, & Tarule 1986, p. 18)

Discovering Girls' Loss of Voice

Laurelei takes her seat in front of the class. It is 10:25 on a January morning in Chicago. Laurelei shivers as she rearranges the black cushion on the chair; is she cold, or is she nervous about sharing her writing in Author's Chair? I shiver too, the room *is* cold, but I *am* nervous about how her piece will be received by her peers. After all, I have been a participant observer in this particular fifth-grade classroom since September, and I have yet to see one of the eleven girls in this room share *anything* in a large group.

1

Laurelei, a ten-year-old Mexican-American, begins to speak: "A Report on Bill Clinton," she says rather quietly. Mr. Roscoe, the classroom teacher, stops her saying, "You're gonna have to be louder." She stumbles and starts again, reading her piece on the presidential inauguration a little more loudly. She does not look up, but her feet, crossed at the ankles, swing back and forth, keeping time as she reads. I look around the room. Many of Laurelei's peers are restless. But Laurelei doesn't notice, and she finishes reading her piece as she began: quietly and nervously.

There is scant applause and Mr. Roscoe opens up the discussion component of Author's Chair (Graves & Hansen 1983) by saying, "Laurelei, *choose* someone." (Students have begun to raise their hands with suggestions, "favorite parts," and questions). Laurelei timidly chooses a boy, who suggests that she put in her piece how Hillary and Bill Clinton met. Mr. Roscoe disagrees, adding, "No, then her piece would be a report on early life." Laurelei again chooses a boy (not one of the remaining ten girls in the class has raised her hand) who wants to know, "What color dress was she [Hillary Clinton] wearing?" This time, Laurelei answers the boy herself, describing in full detail the powder blue dress that Hillary had worn. As no more hands are raised, Mr. Roscoe signals the end of Author's Chair by suggesting to Laurelei that they need to have a content conference to "straighten out some of the order of events." Again, the class applauds quietly, and Laurelei returns to her seat.

As the students then line up for lunch, I place myself alongside the girls' line to talk to them about this event: a girl sharing her writing in Author's Chair. I tell Laurelei what a nice job she did, but she only hangs her head and smiles. Some of the other girls, when I ask as I have asked in the past, tell me again why they will never share their pieces in a large group and why they rarely ask questions of the author in that large group. "My stuff isn't good enough," "I'm too afraid," "What would I ask?" and "Nobody would think it was very important."

Contexts and Rationale

Mr. Roscoe's fifth-grade classroom is situated in a poor, urban neighborhood in Chicago's near-northwest side. "Near-Northwest"* Elementary school serves children who come from a wide variety of ethnic and racial backgrounds, including African American, Anglo American, Latino (Cuban, Puerto Rican, Mexican, Guatemalan) and recent immigrants from Poland and the former USSR. The school's largest population consists of Latinos who comprise well over 50% of the student population.

Considered one of the poorest schools in the city, poverty seems to exacerbate other difficulties (limited English-language status, single-parent homes) that these young students face. For example, close to 100% of the student population qualifies for the state subsidized lunch program, giving evidence to the fact that the community population as a whole falls below the national poverty line set by the United States government.

One of the major challenges, however, that these students faced was *within* the school walls. Near-Northwest was extremely overcrowded as a result of the school district's efforts to "redistribute" and "rebalance" numbers of students throughout the city. Yet, among Mr. Roscoe's colleagues, the common assessment of this phenomenon was that the overflow of students Near-Northwest received was comprised of the students nobody wanted; a sort of Haitian boat people scenario among this city's schoolchildren.

These beliefs were mirrored by attitudes on the "outside" too, as an insidious and dark cloud hung over the city's public education system fueled, in large part, by then-secretary of Education William Bennett's comments some years earlier stating that Chicago had the worst schools in the nation. There was simply a general feeling among many residents of the city that there was no sense to helping these schools; these children simply could not be "saved."

---

*For reasons of confidentiality, the school name, the teacher's name, and all the girls' names are pseudonyms.

This sense that poor urban students were being "dumped" and could not be "saved" was chronicled by teachers and researchers alike (Kozol 1991) and reflected the increasing disdain society in general held toward the poor. Exacerbated by reports of welfare abuse, dropout rates, and violent crime, politicians were able to speak to society's worst fears: the poor would tear down whole cities and educational systems, leaving total destruction in their wake.

Poor girls and women, in particular, are often blamed for this urban decline by a society that expects them to be responsible and accountable for themselves, their families and communities. When they do not behave in a way that "mainstream" society dictates (i.e., maintenance of middle-class values and standards within a nuclear family setting) they are "punished." And their punishment in recent years has become more vicious—moving from such public disdain and distrust to cutting of assistance in health care, child care, and education.

It was in this particular moment of urban public school education that I came to Near-Northwest Elementary school, hoping to give testimony to the promises and potential of urban education, rather than adding to the debate over the challenges and failure of urban public education. With this deeply embedded in my mind, I began a study in Mr. Roscoe's classroom in April 1991 and remained there as a participant observer for several years at the teacher's invitation. Specifically, I had come to Near-Northwest school to observe how non-native speakers participated in peer writing conferences (Blake 1992) and if, as a result of "talking" in these conferences, made substantial revisions to their written pieces. (I was able to report that regardless of native language, students participated fully in conferences and wrote prolifically). What I hadn't noticed, however, was that I had focused my work mainly around the boys' conferences. I hadn't noticed that usually only girls conferenced with girls. I hadn't noticed that girls wrote about certain topics like family responsibilities, altering their voices to fit the public audience of peer conferences and other writing workshop activities. And I hadn't noticed that as the year went on, the girls became increasingly silent and withdrawn from many of the daily classroom activities.

The focus of this book is a study of voice through writing among poor, urban, pre-adolescent fifth-grade girls. Voice became a central focus of this work when, during this earlier study of peer writing conferences I have mentioned, I began to notice what I thought was the girls' loss of voice. This "loss of voice" was apparent through the girls' increased silence in conferences, oral discussions I had with the girls around their writing and other topics, conversations the girls had with each other to which I was privy, and their written pieces, including notes and stories created for both private and public use. Because there were only eleven girls out of a total of twenty-eight students in this present inquiry, the issue of voice became even more crucial, as the girls' voices were quite often, literally, drowned out altogether. The challenges for these young women began in the classroom, and it was here, I believed, that promises and potential could be made and found.

Writing and Voice

Writing is a major means through which girls can begin to integrate what Gilligan (1990) calls formal educational experiences with powerful, personal learning experiences. Because all language is social (Halliday 1978), writing becomes a social activity in which a community of writers interacts to negotiate and construct meaning. Writing, although social, is yet personal, and is inextricably bound to one's culture (Bakhtin 1981, 1986; Burke-LeFevre 1987). Indeed, according to Willinsky (1990) students can shape, construct, and reconstruct their lives experiences as their voices receive an "elevated status" through and by their writing. For example, Shuman (1986) describes how writing allowed the urban adolescent girls in her study a way to work out ideas and problems in the midst of their ongoing experiences. Writing helped them to express their voices as they learned to write and talk about what was important in their lives.

Voice is an elusive, complex, and controversial concept. To writing classroom researchers (Atwell 1987; Calkins 1983, 1986; Graves 1983; Murray 1968), for example, voice is central to the process of writing itself. Expressing "effectively" one's voice becomes the primary avenue in achieving ownership and control of one's writing while students are given opportunities to learn the value and purpose of peer review and collaboration, shared knowledge, and community. Students who are "successful" in moving back and forth among the recursive stages of the process of writing are more willing to revise and edit, produce pieces that exhibit higher textual readability, and develop one's voice. Only recently, however, have writing theorists (Bakhtin 1981, 1986; Dyson 1993; Gilbert 1989; Lensmire 1993, 1994) addressed how and why a writing process approach becomes the site for significant tension and struggle over issues like ownership and voice.

For Bakhtin (1981, 1986) the entire process of writing is charged with emotion and struggle over meaning, value, and voice. Multiple, socio-historical voices collide in this struggle and it is a very difficult task for the writer to sort out, organize, and express these competing voices in writing. This becomes especially difficult for girls, for example, as they search for voices of their own among the multiple voices they hear and know.

In Mr. Roscoe's classroom the girls exhibited multiple voices as they wrote and talked about their lives. In public writing contexts such as writing workshop activities, the girls shared their writing, albeit reluctantly, with their peers and with Mr. Roscoe. It wasn't until a quarter of the way through the school year that the girls began to include me in their repertoire of private writing activities, such as note writing and oral texts they created around fights, for example. It was here, outside of the public sphere of classroom writing, that a plethora of writing was taking place. It was here that I began to hear voices that were distinctly different from the voices I heard expressed in public. And it was

here that the girls' voices resounded with critical issues they
wished to be addressed.

This book, in an attempt to describe the multiple voices
of eleven girls in Mr. Roscoe's classroom through their writing, also seeks to fill a large gap in the current research
and in current prevailing attitudes about urban public education in general. Through a close and detailed study of
these girls' voices, we can begin to move toward a more positive yet critical analysis of the struggles and hopes of poor,
urban pre-adolescent girls, leading us toward curricular and
attitudinal changes that seek to speak to the *success* of
urban, public education, rather than to its failure. It is
hoped that these voices will educate and enrich others' lives
as they have enriched mine.

Overview of the Book

Chapter 2 begins a discussion around language and
language choice, particularly as choice relates to power,
prestige, and resistance. In this fifth-grade classroom, I
learned not only how I was defined and redefined by language, but also how the boys, for example, used particular
language to control and remain more powerful over the
girls. Language choice, and resistance to language choice,
then, became a crucial prerequisite for voice among the girls
in Mr. Roscoe's classroom.

Chapter 3 addresses more fully the theoretical constructs of voice. Central to this discussion will be an examination of what is meant by "multiple voices" and how
attempting to sort out and express multiple voices can
become, at the same time, both a dilemma and a survival
technique for girls in particular.

Chapter 4 consists of two parts. The first part begins by
describing not only the various contexts, both public and
private, in which the girls wrote but also the genres, topics,
and themes the girls chose for their writing. The second
part focuses on the girls themselves as, mostly through their
own writing, they are described. It is here that the girls'

linguistic heritages, family backgrounds, and interests both in and out of school are revealed.

In chapter 5, I explore the writing workshop as the major "public" avenue by which girls could write and express their voices. Specifically, chapter 4's focus is on the non-fiction pieces the girls created for public use and the influences from literature that supported the girls' inquiry and resultant texts. Chapter 6's focus, too, is on pieces created within the public context of the writing workshop. Here, however, I examine the narrative and fictional pieces the girls created for public use and the influences from popular literature, for example, that helped to shape these stories.

Chapter 7 explores more closely the private contexts that Mr. Roscoe and I created for the girls to expand and express personal voices through writing. Specifically, this chapter focuses on three pervasive themes on which the girls most often chose to write: domesticity, family life, and sexuality. Chapter 8 also examines the girls' writing through more private contexts. Influences from popular culture such as television, rap music, families, and school will be examined through their writing and their talk around their writing. The increasing and insidious influence of violence is also discussed in these latter contexts.

Chapter 9 begins an initial exploration of the necessity of providing a critical response to what I have called the "cultural texts" and thus, the voices, of the girls as they write. Some of the boys' voices are introduced here to highlight the very powerful influence their voices have on the girls, Mr. Roscoe, and even myself, as we learned to move toward a critical response of the girls' texts and voices.

The final chapter of this book, chapter 10, explores future directions of this research in relation to the efficacy of a process writing approach and on the necessity of a critical response both by students and the teacher to girls' multiple voices. A central focus for the discussion and implications, then, is how girls' multiple voices need to be included into the classroom writing curriculum.

The overall goal of this study was to reveal and document the struggles and tensions poor, urban girls experi-

ence and how these struggles and tensions could be explored
through various contexts within a classroom writing setting.
Poor, urban girls' voices have not been adequately represented in research, and to that end, it is hoped this work
can contribute to discussions surrounding improved education for all students, but especially for those students who
have little power. Through language and the written word,
poor, urban, pre-adolescent girls express their voices as they
learn to resist and challenge other voices, creating their own.
If heard, and critically responded to, these multiple voices
can become powerful voices on the edge of adolescence.

2

Language and the Woman with the Yellow Hair:
Perspectives on Language Choice and Use

It has been said that the most important intellectual
achievement of any human life is learning a first language . . . we all enter school speaking a first language. In
school we find out its name. A child who has learned to
speak a nonstandard form has learned as much about
how to learn a language as the child who has learned a
standard one; that learning to learn has to be conserved.
(Bateson 1994, p. 206)

Some years ago, while attending a lecture by the late
Toni Cade Bambara at a local university, a discussion
ensued where Ms. Bambara began to speak of language
"markers" that we use to label and categorize people.
Markers were used, she said, to save ourselves from thinking. A woman from the audience, seemingly confused, then
asked Ms. Bambara to give her an idea of what to call "low-
income, non-mainstream, African-Americans." Toni Cade
Bambara, quickly and with what appeared to be without a
second thought, replied, "Call them what they call themselves: poor Blacks." "That's what they are," she said, dif-
fusing and dismissing the sighs and gasps that could be
heard among the predominately white, middle and upper-
middle class academic crowd. Later, as I got to know Mr.
Roscoe's students, I learned that, indeed, these students
called *themselves* "poor" and "Black," a fact that was first
brought to my attention when some of the girls talked about

how poor they were because they went to a "cheap" school where there was no nurse on staff.

Language markers are a social tool. That is, we use language to learn about and become socialized into our families, cultures, and society. We use language to communicate, to express thoughts, and to respond to others' thoughts. We learn languages in what Dyson (1995) calls "other people's contexts" (p. 325) within which we can negotiate, respond, create, and recreate.

Language is also a political tool. That is, we use language to persuade, to challenge, and to monitor and control the messages we give and receive. We learn at a very early age (albeit, perhaps, unconsciously or subliminally) of the potentials of language to silence and to suppress. We learn whose language counts, and who uses the language that counts and in what contexts. We also learn how to separate and resist through language.

Language has been, historically, an effective weapon to separate the "mainstream" from the "non-mainstream;" to delineate the self from the "Other." In this particular historical moment, language used by the mainstream is increasingly controlled, monitored, and employed by a select few people who can manipulate symbols, words, and texts. This manipulation is strictly governed by a "standard" code of what constitutes the mainstream language. And yet, the non-mainstream *resist* through language, a resistance clearly seen, for example, in the use of "non-standard," non-mainstream dialects, codes, and texts of urban, poor students such as those in Mr. Roscoe's fifth-grade classroom.

The purpose of this chapter is to highlight two key, interrelated points around some of the word and language choices both I and the girls in Mr. Roscoe's classroom made and use throughout this text. First, I wish to show how my position as a "mainstream" white woman was both defined and redefined by our language choices. That is, the self-Other marker (See Appendix B for a fuller discussion around the "self-Other" distinction) I so often struggled with, was indeed, constantly shaped and reshaped by the interactions, negotiations, and responses to and through the language choices we made. And second, because of this constant redefinition and recreation of language markers through and by our language choices, I will show how the girls learned to be more bold in negotiating, resisting, and in attempting to have their voices heard. I conclude this chapter by providing a brief list of some of the other, perhaps less controversial, words and phrases I have chosen to represent the girls and the contexts in which they went to school and live.

The Woman with the Yellow Hair: Redefining the "Mainstream"

Originally trained as a linguist, I came to Mr. Roscoe's classroom with the strong belief that there was nothing less contentious nor political than language choice and use, particularly among those who were separated (i.e., whether by culture, race, gender, age, or socioeconomic class) from the mainstream and, therefore, the "standard." I knew, then, of the potentially powerful role of language in the experience and expression of the girls' culture, and saw language as the most important way in which these urban girls could articulate their cultural, racial, gender, and age identities. What I did not initially see, nor understand however, was how my own language use served to "correct" or even to suppress theirs. In other words, simply by being an "outsider" who was white and middle class, I could be (and was) identified by many of the standard codes of the mainstream. That is, anytime I opened my mouth and spoke, I potentially positioned the girls as the "Other," as my words, *by their very nature*, exerted my authority and reminded the girls of my more privileged position.

Yet, I also did not immediately recognize why and how the girls used their language (and thus, non-standard codes) as a tool of resistance. That is, although, for example, the girls were unable to articulate a sense of self-Other, they were certainly able (and quickly did so) to establish boundaries and roles vis-à-vis difference. Since mine was a culture that so very clearly defined these young women as not only "minority" but poor and uneducable and theirs was one that looked at mine with disdain and distrust, terms of difference, and even suspicion formed the initial base for comparing our different cultures. Their language use emphasized this distrust, as it seemed to be intended to surprise and shock me, highlighting and maintaining our distance even further. To do this, they not only used language to identify me as different, but also used particular language (often unfamiliar to me) to remind me of this separation. For example, words and phrases that brought attention to my different physical characteristics, including my skin and hair color (e.g., the woman with the "yellow hair") were commonplace.

Language as Resistance

The girls' language choices were indeed tools of resistance, resistance that later was reflected in the texts they struggled to create and share.

One way in which the girls resisted, making what I considered to be culturally and age-different language choices was in the trick notes that they wrote (see chapter 7). These notes were aptly named by the girls because they were used to "trick" a particular boy in the class to think a (made-up) girl were interested in him sexually. The girls accomplished this by using such explicitly sexual language as "dick," "pussy," and "fuck."

This kind of "shocking" language, too, could be heard in the responses the girls used to the fierce name-calling they were subject to by the boys, and in the lyrics of rap music all the students listened to; lyrics that were clearly used to delineate (and make problematic) our different social classes, racial/ethnic groups, and our ages, but also the girls' place and roles in their own communities. As I spent more time, though, listening to the kinds of language the girls' used, negotiated, rejected, and resisted with, in *particular contexts*, I came to the realization that these very conscious choices served other purposes: purposes unspoken, and thereby, unacknowledged.

For example, as curious and offensive as I (initially) found the use of words such as "bitch," "white nigger," and "pussy," it became far more interesting and frightening to me that the girls seemed to accept the use of such language even when it directly assaulted them. As I began to understand that this language was not necessarily directed at me, but rather at the boys, or even at society (i.e., white society) in general, I too saw that this apparent acceptance of these language choices was actually a form of resistance, of "taking back" language that was used to directly assault and insult them. This became even more salient as the girls and I began to talk increasingly about particular language choices and the potential effects of learning to negotiate in making (and accepting) these choices.

When we first began meeting on a regular basis in writers' circle (see chapter 4 for a detailed description of "writers' circle"), the girls and I not only negotiated topics and themes on which we could write, but also words and terms we could use in our writing. We collectively decided that "vulgar" words like "dick" and "asshole" could be replaced by other words like "jerk" and "pain in the butt." Obviously, these alternative words did not carry the same impact as some of the girls' original choices, nor did they help them to declare their resistance. They did, however, carry less of a stigma (i.e., according to the standard language/code of mainstream society) and therefore, we agreed, could only help the girls' position in being taken seriously, and most crucially, *in having their voices heard* through their writing in the public contexts of the classroom. And although many of the girls continued to insist they would continue to use vulgarity as a form of protest to the boys (whom, the girls knew, used these words to not only describe them but also to categorize and control them), they too began to understand the potentially powerful role in being able to negotiate and make different language choices to make the space for their voices to be heard.

Language as Thought

The language choices I have made throughout this book to describe the girls and the contexts in which they wrote were first and foremost chosen so that their voices were not further silenced nor suppressed. Yet, as importantly, my language choices reflect the direct and powerful influence the *girls'* choices of language had on me. Our initial lack of understanding of each other became a common understanding, particularly around gender or "sisterhood" where terms of endearment centered on familiar markers: low self-esteem, resistance, and lack of voice. In other words, what I initially believed was an intent "to shock" was really a desire to share and to be heard.

I am not suggesting, however, that one word may be "better" than another, nor am I suggesting that *I* know better which words or markers are more "accurate" or "correct." My choices I hope do suggest that I believe it crucial that both students and teachers pay considerable thought to their word and language choices, understanding that language is fluid and complex, ever-changing, negotiated, created, and should be reflective of the care we take in not only making choices about the words and terms we choose, but also in making choices about how we then use those words. (See Nieto 1992, for a similar perspective on language choice and thought).

Following is a short, non-exhaustive list of some of the other words that you will find used throughout this book; words, I hope, that are indeed reflective of the care I have spoken about here:

Urban vs. Inner City:

I have chosen to use the word "urban" rather than "inner city" for one primary reason. The term "urban" carries much less of a negative connotation than does "inner city," i.e., the word designates an *area* rather than a *condition*.

Girls vs. Young Women:

I initially found this choice to be a fairly simple one. By virtue of their age, I thought, the girls in Mr. Roscoe's class-

room were just that: girls. Yet, if the term "woman" is a
state of mind that exudes a sense of responsibility and
maturity (rather than an indication of age) then many of
the girls in his classroom would be considered young
women. (See chapters 7 and 8 for a fuller discussion on the
nature and scope of many of these girls' responsibilities.)

African-American vs. Black:

Although virtually every student I spoke to in the school
used the term "Black," I have chosen to use "African-
American" in this book. As I spent more and more time among
Mr. Roscoe's students, however, my choice became more and
more curious to me as I began to wonder if I just weren't following a "politically correct" academic protocol that had no
meaning nor value to the students. I have remained faithful to
my choice of "African American" here, even amidst the strong
images that my using it in front of the students always con-
jures up; images of them laughing or crinkling up their noses
at me, trying to figure out why I often talked "so funny."

Angla vs. White:

I have interchanged the use of these two terms. I have
tried to justify my choices about these words by saying that
Latinos are much more likely to use "Anglo," whereas African-
Americans (and Whites) are much more likely to use "White."
Upon closer reflection, however, I believe now that a large part
of my decision to interchange these words was my own fear—a
fear of being labeled something I was not so comfortable with.

Latina vs. Hispanic:

This choice just made sense from a socio-linguistic
point of view: not all Spanish speakers are "Hispanic" and
therefore should not be labeled as such.

Language Use and Redefining the Mainstream

Language is indeed a social and political tool by which
people are defined, categorized, and controlled. Even with my

background in languages and linguistics, I felt threatened by certain terms and words the girls in Mr. Roscoe's class used on a regular basis, being (initially) particularly disturbed when I assumed that the language was directed at me. In this chapter, I have highlighted not only why my choices and the girl's choices of words and terms were important, but also how both our choices reshaped attitudes toward each other—as, for example, "girlfriend" became the ultimate compliment; a term that helped me to know that on some level, I had reached "insider" status with the girls in Mr. Roscoe's classroom and a term that helped the girls to know I was listening.

There are two important lessons to be remembered as this book unfolds and is reflected upon. First, the word "mainstream" is really a metaphor for language employed by those who have power to control through language. In this instance, the mainstream accomplish this by affording themselves a particular status different from and superior to those labeled, "non-mainstream." Second, because language *is* used to control, it shapes thought, which in turn shapes perspectives and perceptions. In other words, the mainstream expects urban girls to get pregnant, for example, as evidenced by a too-frequently held attitude like the teacher who, during lunch among her colleagues and myself, exclaimed (about a well-known girl in the school): "Well, listen to her mouth, you know she's headed for trouble, she'll be pregnant by the end of the year."

The "mainstream" controls the "standard" because they maintain power over it. Learning to negotiate meaning as well as learning to understand others' uses and purposes for language is a first, crucial step in allowing others, e.g., the "non-mainstream" to express their voices in an honest and convincing way. And it is an absolutely critical step in learning to listen to the non-mainstream voices and to incorporate those voices, too, into the daily lessons of both school and life.

Summary

Language is a powerful tool that is essential not only for communication, but also for expression, negotiation and understanding, power, control, and resistance. Yet, too, as language is a prerequisite or a "necessary condition" for voice, language is not voice. In the next chapter, I examine more closely the theoretical underpinnings of "voice" along with its relationship and resistance to language and language choice, particularly to those choices that have been created by those who "empower" or "give voice" to others.

3

Multiple Voices:
Expressing and Responding to the
Language of Voice Through Writing

Language has a life of its own—it exists even when it is
suppressed; when voice is suppressed, it is not heard—it
does not exist. (Ruiz 1991, p. 220)

Girls' doubling of voice and vision is a response to [a] situation—to becoming at once inside and outside of the
world they are entering as young women. And this dizzy-
ing ability to see and to speak in two ways also enables
girls to resist the pressures and the temptations they face
simply to fit themselves into the world in which they are
living by taking on a male perspective. (Gilligan 1993,
p. 148)

Language and Voice

Language represents a "central force in the struggle
for voice" (Giroux 1986, cited in Ruiz, p. 218). Language
allows for voice, language can shape voice; language can
even proclaim voice. But, language is not voice. Language,
in fact, may only be the medium in which we express voice;
it may not adequately reflect our "inner resources" (Belenky
et al. 1986, p. 54).

Ruiz (1991) makes this point clearly, when talking
about the difference between choice of language among non-
native speakers of English and voice through language:
"When sociolinguists carry out their investigations of lan-

guage use, they ask, 'Who says what to whom in what language?' When we investigate the issue of voice, we should ask, 'Who says?'" (p. 220). In other words, having the opportunity to use the *medium* (language) to express oneself does not ensure one is, in reality, given the *agency* (voice) to truly reflect one's inner self.

An interpretation of voice is problematic for a number of reasons. First, too often, voice is equated with "empowerment" or "cultural identity" (Cummins 1986; Ferdman 1990). Here, the implicit assumption holds that by *giving* students the opportunity to bring in their personal experiences, they can move closer to their true cultural identity; thus, being empowered, or given voice, by the teacher or experience. Voice, then, in this view, becomes something that someone (teacher) can give to someone else (student).

Ferdman's (1990) central thesis rests on just that notion: students (especially those from what he calls "minority" backgrounds) can be "empowered" by being "permitted to discover and explore ethnic connections" (p. 200). However, Ferdman does not address the notion that even when diverse cultures and languages become "recognized and appreciated," it does not ensure that this diversity is expressed by the students in an honest and meaningful way. In short, it does not ensure the students' voice.

As Ruiz (1991) has argued, the interpretation of voice is a crucial notion that needs to be addressed more closely and more critically. It is one thing for teachers (and others) to claim they are "empowering" or "giving voice" to their students; quite another for the voices to be truly heard. For Ruiz, "to have a voice implies not just that people can say things, but that they are heard" (p. 220).

Delpit (1986; 1988) also makes problematic the issue of whether, indeed, one can empower or give voice to others. Too often, she claims, "a certain paternalism creeps into the speech of some of our liberal colleagues as they explain that our children must be 'given voice'" (1986, p. 384). Instead, she says, all educators must realize that there are other voices; there is always another voice found in every student that needs to be reached and expressed.

The second major reason an interpretation of voice becomes problematic comes from socio-constructivist writing theory (Bakhtin 1981, 1986; Cazden 1988; Dyson 1993; Lensmire 1993, 1994; Pappas 1993). Primarily, these theorists argue that language is *never* a neutral medium, devoid of socio-cultural and historical contexts that traditional theory suggests. Rather, language is developed and expressed through a wide range of contexts and experiences, contexts that are always present and always changing. Language, therefore, is not only "marked with the voices of prior contexts" (Pappas 1993, p. 26) but also with the voices of present situations. In other words, there is always a multitude of, often, competing, contradictory voices emanating through a text. These voices are the voices of intent, experience, knowledge, and opinion.

It is the focus of this chapter to explore various issues around an interpretation of voice. This interpretation of voice comes from many fields that offer many perspectives. Here, however, I offer perspectives from women writers, the literature of girls' psychology, feminist studies, and writing research. It is through this interdisciplinary approach to an understanding of voice and its implications for girls in particular in an urban writing setting, that I believe the nature of voice as complex, controversial, and often contradictory can best be examined.

Voice and a Room of One's Own

There has been a long tradition of women writers who explored the development of voice through writing. Virginia Woolf struggled with this fundamental issue of voice through writing, and who, of course, lost the struggle (or perhaps won it?) when she killed herself in the 1960s. In her treatise on women and fiction, Woolf (1929) poses the question, "What effect has poverty on fiction?" (p. 25). Here, Woolf means not only the poverty of material goods, but the poverty of one's creativity and expression; the poverty, certainly, of voice. Without voice, Woolf tells us, a woman is

". . . so thwarted and hindered by other people, so tortured and pulled asunder by her own contrary instincts, that she must [have lost] lose her health and sanity to a certainty" (p. 51).

The ability, however, to be able to create and to be heard through one's writing, allows for an amelioration of these effects of "poverty" as women, too, find "the submerged truth" through this release of expression through the written word. If a woman is to write, Woolf concludes, she "must have money and a room of one's own" (p. 4). Women must have the space and time to write, the space and time to reflect on their lives' experiences, and the "intellectual freedom" granted others in this society to do so.

The struggle for a voice and a "room of one's own" among female writers can be found in Gilman's work at the turn of the century as well. Lane (1980) describes for us the struggles and "madness" of the young woman (author of the "The Yellow Wallpaper" in 1892) who, like the women in Gilman's fictional world, struggled to "reach a new sense of themselves . . . usually through their work" (p. 39). These characters, like Gilman, we learn, searched for one's voice through work and writing amidst great risk. We are reminded of the hardship and "unbearable . . . elements" in Gilman's "inner and outer life" which, "unspeakable" in contemporary society, were ultimately "managed . . . through [her] fiction" (p. 41). Gilman, too, in the face of great risk, found solace, and some sense of voice, through her writing.

In contemporary literature, Morrison (Micucci 1992), too, tells of her struggle with "poverty" and a "room of one's own" as she, like many women, created and wrote "privately at night [like women] with families who use their off hours for creative projects" (p. 3). She, too, searched for a voice through these stolen moments that would allow her to explore not only issues of gender and race, but also to explore her identity as a woman and the possibilities of self and being human in the world. According to Morrison, writing allows one to "stretch and grow deeper" because the "search for love and identity runs through everything [I write]" (p. 3). Writing is also a place where "one can be

courageous" and "think the unthinkable" (p. 3). Indeed,
according to Heilbrun (Matthews 1992) a contemporary feminist writer and scholar, "life and literature are linked . . .
we are the stories we tell" (p. 83).

The implications these writers' words hold for the issue
of writing and voice, especially among girls like the eleven
in Mr. Roscoe's classroom are profound. Girls need permission in the classroom to write. In a classroom where this
permission is "given," writing may be the major avenue
through which young women can begin to integrate what
Gilligan (1990) calls formal educational experiences with
powerful learning experiences.

Gender, Writing, and Voice

According to Gilligan (1990), it is absolutely crucial at
the early adolescent stage (usually considered to begin
around the fifth-grade or ten years of age) for girls not to
separate formal education from powerful learning experiences. As young women learn to deal with evolving emotional issues such as connection and relationship, and learn
to deal with the perceived validity of these evolving emotions, they require guidance, role models, and confirmation
to further their emotional development. Instead, however,
because formal education has traditionally centered on
other issues—i.e., autonomy, independence, detachment,
and separation, pre-adolescent girls not only begin to
"observe where and when women speak and when they are
silent" (Gilligan 1990, p. 25), but also begin to learn precisely how to separate formal educational experiences from
their other learning experiences. In other words, girls learn,
and internalize, that what they consider to be central to
their learning and knowledge lies, in fact, outside of any
formal school realm. Girls understand that the image of the
nice girl is so persuasive that they learn to modulate,
silence, or appropriate others' voices altogether.

Feminist researchers (Belenky et al. 1986; Gilligan
1982, 1990; Gilbert, 1989, 1991; Fine, 1987, 1991) see an

appropriation of voice as extremely problematic for girls. Because girls have traditionally held few positions from which to speak (Gilbert 1989), they typically learn to do what these researchers have called "doubling" their voices. This doubling of voice is considered to be a direct response to a situation of a "deeply-knotted dilemma of being at once inside and outside of the world they are entering as young women" (Gilligan 1993, p. 148). In other words, girls feel they must present separate voices depending on the context, audience, purpose, and theme for both speaking and writing.

Fine's (1987) work among urban adolescent girls supports the notion that girls learn to develop two or more separate voices. "Good" girls trained themselves to speak and produce in two voices, one academic, and one at the margin. While the academic voice was one that denied class, gender, and race and "reproduced ideologies about hard work, success, and their 'natural' sequence; and stifled the desire to disrupt" (p. 163), the marginal voice expressed more private experiences and struggles such as those that *revolved around* discussions of gender, race, and class. This particular two voice dilemma was often more permanently resolved by "creative, if ultimately self-defeating strategies" (p. 164) like dropping out of school.

Researchers (Belenky et al. 1986; Bell 1991; Fine 1991; Gilligan 1990; Lewis 1988, 1990; Sassen 1980; Weis 1991) report that girls as young as elementary age exhibit similar self-defeating strategies. Too often, even at this young age, girls realize (and can articulate) that success and voice are mutually exclusive, simply because they are female. Indeed, according to Fine (1991), girls learn quickly that the price of academic success is the "muting" of one's own voice.

Bell (1991) supports the notion that even elementary age girls can articulate a success/voice dichotomy, which is further compounded by race, socioeconomic class, and ethnicity:

> Success is a loaded experience for females in this culture and embodies a myriad of conflicting feelings, values, and

cultural messages about gender, race, ~~and class. Girls~~
receive contradictory messages about success from a com-
petitively oriented society that on the one hand claims
that females can be and do anything, but on the other
promotes the belief that females should be 'feminine,' 'pas-
sive,' and protected from risk. (p. 238)

Muting one's voice is a phenomenon that can be found
among females at the secondary and the college level as
well (Lewis & Simon 1986; Lewis 1988; Lewis 1990; Weis
1991). At the high school level, girls begin, often, to show
"feminist glimmerings" (Weis 1991). However, these same
young women become "thwarted" in their attempts toward a
personal or collective voice, as they often learn that there is
no model on which to extend a potentially "critical moment
of critique of male dominance and patriarchy" (Weis, p. 99).
In fact, Brown & Gilligan (1992) report that it is precisely
the lack of female role models in particular that help to
thwart these efforts. Adult women practice what Brown &
Gilligan (1992) refer to as "voice training" that, when modeled by adult "good" women, "undermines [these] girls' experiences with what others say is reality" (p. 61). Young
women at the high school level learn that there are very
few avenues in which they can explore their identities as
females. They learn precisely how *not* to challenge existing
male-dominated notions of identity within a school setting
as they also learn that there are very few adult female role
models who are willing to step out of the "good girl" mode
and speak or support their own voices. For the eleven girls
in Mr. Roscoe's classroom these issues became more complex as gender perspectives are always mediated by race,
ethnicity, and class.

The silence of the voices of young women is also
reported at the university level (Lewis & Simon 1986; Lewis
1990). As a graduate student, Lewis (in Lewis & Simon
1986) reports that the "overwhelming experience [women
experience throughout their education and lives] ... is that of
being silenced" (p. 459). Women, Lewis claims, have
"accepted the powerlessness," by the time they reach this

level, of being able to "define a discourse within which we
can speak . . . [resulting in] an act that forfeits our voice . . ."
(p. 462). Voice and gender, then, becomes a personal and
political statement; something that cannot be singularly
understood.

Multiple Voices in Mr. Roscoe's Classroom

No single voice can speak for [women's] multiple experiences. Central to a discussion of voice, then, is the issue of
how to honor girls' *multiple* voices as they learn to express
them through writing. It becomes critical in the classroom to
find ways to incorporate all of the girls' other, multiple
voices as voices that count.

The notion of voice through writing is dependent on
the larger pedagogical contexts of the classroom; public writing contexts that are often firmly situated within a learned,
dominant discourse, and private writing contexts that are
situated within other, multiple discourses.

For girls, writing and voice *is* a learned discourse,
"learned as a the result of taking up particular positions
within discourses . . . [which are] gendered positions"
(Gilbert 1989, p. 261). These gendered positions then are
reflected in girls' searches for voice. This search signifies
both compliance and resistance to the dominant discourse of
voice as girls begin to incorporate or appropriate voices from
this dominant discourse.

The eleven girls in Mr. Roscoe's classroom expressed
distinct voices from one context to the next. The girls
often wrote about the same sorts of concerns (through
various themes) but with different expressions of voice.
The girls understood and utilized certain voices, what the
research here has called a doubling of voice, a muting of
voice, and an appropriation of voice. These girls also
expressed multiple voices: voices dependent on context
and genre, audience and author; voices that were always
complex, often contradictory, reluctant, resistant, false,
fearful, and hopeful.

Summary

Voice is a complex and often contradictory notion. Research has clearly shown that most girls do not (and do not know how to) express voices of their own. Rather, they incorporate learned strategies such as muting their voices, silencing their voices, and/or doubling their voices for different contexts and for different audiences. Encouraging girls' multiple voices as voices that count along with learning to critically respond to these multiple voices, then, become critical factors in helping girls, in particular, to express and develop voices of their own.

4

Setting the Stage:
Classroom Writing Contexts and
Brief Introductions to Eleven Girls

The process model, insofar as it facilitates and legitimizes the expression of the individual voice, is compatible with the feminist revisioning of hierarchy, if not essential to it . . . Writing . . . has the potential to be the single most important learning experience for [girls] if it provides them the confidence in their own ideas and belief in their own authority. (Caywood & Overing 1987, xiv–xv)

Various Writing Contexts in Mr. Roscoe's Classroom

The contexts in which the eleven girls wrote in Mr. Roscoe's classroom varied, as did the purposes, genres, topics they chose to write as well as the audience for whom they chose to share their writing. The purpose of this chapter is to describe these various contexts, purposes, genres, topics, and audiences, and then to introduce the eleven girls and their voices through their own writing.

Purpose in writing is synonymous to "intention." In a socio-constructive perspective on writing, purpose, intent, genre, topic choice, and context are interrelated. Here, for clarification purposes, however, I explain them each in turn. A student may write to fulfill a teacher's requirement, to be included in a peer conference, or to relay information to a friend, e.g., through passing notes. Purpose and intention focus on the "why" and "involves a particular understanding of relationships between sender and recipient . . . and combines form of production with form of exchange" (Shuman 1986, pp. 96–97). For example, the girls in Mr. Roscoe's class wrote to protest injustices, to complain about victimization, or to simply communicate a story from home from one friend to another.

The term genre is *typically* associated with the *type* of text that one produces, integrally tied to the social intent or purpose of writing, and each genre carries rules for appropriate use. The most familiar genre to pre-adolescents is probably the narrative, but other types of text, such as persuasive essays, expository reports, and poetry are evident within students' experimentation with written text. Topic is the "theme" or "subject" of the text which the student is writing. Topic choice is one of the cornerstones of a process writing pedagogy and varies widely within a process writing classroom. Students are encouraged to choose their own topics, to become "vested" in their work, to "own" the meaning of their writing.

Context describes circumstances in which a particular event occurs. Such a definition, however, seems lacking. Writing workshop was the largest and most encompassing *public* context within which the girls wrote. However, context also includes the contexts or the influences on the girls' writing from their backgrounds and experiences. The term context here, then, is much like the notion of multiple meanings and voice that I have discussed in previous chapters. That is, even though I talk about one or two "large" (i.e., one public, one private) contexts in which the girls wrote, always present are the underlying contexts of culture that affect very profoundly not only how the young girls perceive writing, but their choice of purpose, genre, and topic. These multiple contexts, then, of course, always influenced profoundly how I and Mr. Roscoe, in turn, perceived their writing.

Thus, context depends crucially on audience. That is, a context becomes relatively appealing or not appealing according to who may then be expected to listen to a piece, for example. According to Lensmire (1994), however, proponents of the writing workshop have seldom considered *critically* the effect audience has on shaping and constraining writing and voice. As I have already indicated, the girls in Mr. Roscoe's classroom not only rarely, if at all, participated in large group share-time activities because of the mostly male audience they were faced with, and when they did share their writing, they clearly tailored their voices to this audience. (See chapters 4 and 5 for samples of this tailoring and a discussion around why the girls altered their voices for public forums). The public sharing of pieces was considered a risky undertaking by the girls and was one of the most salient factors for the girls in deciding how to express their voices and for whom.

In Mr. Roscoe's process writing classroom, genre and topic choice were usually left to the student. Mr. Roscoe, through thematic units around such subjects as "SPACE" and "LEADERS," encouraged students to write a range of non-fictional genres including informational ones. He also introduced genres such as poetry and persuasive writing, and modeling the process one might use to begin composing such genres.

The Public Sphere of Writing Workshop

The writing workshop was the context in which much of the girls' in-school writing was expected to take place. Writing produced around writing workshop activities "counted," i.e., for grades, for group discussion while writing outside of the writing workshop often did not. Moreover, pieces created during writing workshop were considered "public." That is, the girls expected that they would have to share some of their pieces in large groups such as Author's Chair, with Mr. Roscoe in content conferences, or with another classmate during peer conferencing.

The writing workshop took place each morning and took a substantial portion of morning classroom time. Mr. Roscoe structured the workshop to include various activities: a mini-lesson, peer-peer conferencing, teacher-student conferencing, and Author's Chair. Mr. Roscoe typically began each morning with a mini-lesson on writing. The topic varied: one day it was on how to do a title page; another day on contractions; still another on revision strategies. By 9:30 a.m. or so, the students began to write.

When students finished drafting pieces they would choose a classmate with whom to conference. The two students would find a corner or empty desk in the room where the author would read her piece. When the author was finished reading, the student "audience" or "critic" offered suggestions on how to make the piece clearer and more interesting. The peer critic took notes for the author and the author was expected to incorporate some or all of the critic's ideas into her second draft. When an author completed a second draft, she often had a content and proofreading conference with Mr. Roscoe. Finally, she began to edit. Finished pieces were often published, read in front of the class, and displayed throughout the room. Developing and expressing one's voice was always encouraged.

Thus, Mr. Roscoe created many opportunities within the writing workshop for the students to write and talk about their writing. In addition to peer-peer conferences, Author's Chair, and teacher/student conferences, Mr. Roscoe was active in promoting other writing activities for public use such as apology note writing. The class, as a whole, wrote numerous notes throughout the year; apologizing to lunchroom attendants, substitute teachers, the principal, other classroom teachers, and even to me. These apology notes served to emphasize the importance of community and group accountability; both of which are integral components of a writing process pedagogy.

Mr. Roscoe also created more private contexts for writing within the classroom. These included letter writing and response journal writing.

Private Writing Contexts Provided by Mr. Roscoe

Letter writing formed a large portion of the girls' private writing experiences. Early in the school year, Mr.

Roscoe enlisted some of his students to help make "mailboxes" for their letter writing within the class. The mailboxes, constructed out of large cardboard boxes (that looked as if they used to hold bottles of wine because of the cardboard separations) made their home in the back of the room where I usually sat. A mailbox was made for me the first week I was there, and it became part of my daily routine to check to see if I, too, had gotten any mail. Mr. Roscoe had a mailbox as well, but his was made of metal with the flag that went up and down on its side. Mr. Roscoe's mailbox sat on his desk, which Mr. Roscoe told me was often full of letters (again mostly from the girls).

Sitting next to the mailboxes in the back of the room gave me a particularly clear perspective on how letter writing was used, and by whom, in the classroom. It was the girls who used the mailboxes far more often. It was the boys who stole or "borrowed" the girls mail far more often. In fact, "borrowing" mail became such a commonplace activity that Mr. Roscoe asked that the class brainstorm and write rules to be posted near the mailboxes. Rules included a "read only your own mail" warning.

Response journals represented another more private writing context that Mr. Roscoe created for his students. Response journals became, at least initially, a place where the girls in particular were most comfortable in sharing information about themselves or their families. Later, they were used at Mr. Roscoe's request, almost exclusively for responses to books the students were reading. Response journals were only read by the student writing the entry, Mr. Roscoe, and myself.

Other Private Writing Contexts

Other private writing contexts were ones that I introduced to the girls. These contexts include writers' circle and journal writing. An additional context includes "oral texts."

I developed writers' circle to allow the girls a chance to write, peer conference, and share their work outside of the context of the writers' workshop, away from Mr. Roscoe and the boys. I felt very strongly that the girls needed a place where they could, indeed, write and talk about what they wished. I had also become concerned that the girls were experiencing a "loss of voice" (see chapter 1) and wished to explore what appeared to be their increasing silence and withdrawal in classroom writing activities. (A discussion of writers' circle as a methodological issue can be found in Appendix A.) The writing we did in this group, however, was not intended to supplant their writing for Mr. Roscoe in writers' workshop, which I made clear in our first meeting. All of the eleven girls, some of whom were nervous at first because they didn't quite know what was expected of them, joined the group. We met once or twice a week in the hallway. Topic choice was left up to the girls and they often brainstormed on the topics in which they, collectively, were most interested. Topics brainstormed in our first meeting included: Boys We Hate, Periods, Babies Who Have Babies, Babies Who Are Born Early, Fifth Grade, and What's Unfair.

Oral texts were an integral, and embedded, format for the girls in writers' circle. Oral texts or everyday discourse can be important bases for girls' writing and their expressions of private voices, precisely because of its proximity to narrative (Shuman 1986). For example, the young adolescent girls that Shuman studied routinely transferred "oral face-to-face exchanges into written exchanges . . . by adapting formulaic patterns of speech to produce written pieces" (p. 121). That is, girls' talk around a topic was sometimes turned into a written text. Among these pre-adolescent girls, however, oral texts were also used to pre-write or brainstorm on topics that were too risky to write about.

In addition, I gave each girl a journal in which to write. This became a problem as the boys were angry at me for not giving them something, and then later, perhaps in retaliation, or pure curiosity, began to steal the girls' journals out of their desks. By the end of the study, four girls had "misplaced" their journals.

All of the eleven girls reported that they kept diaries at home. No one ever shared her diary with me, attesting to the fact that this writing context was, indeed, perhaps the most private and personal. There was, however, a lot of discussion around the fact that this writing had to be hidden for fear that male siblings would find the diaries, read them, and tell all the world.

Summary

Various writing contexts were provided for the girls to write. These contexts affected not only what the girls wrote, but how, and for whom. The girls were given ample opportunities to write to express their voices around self-selected topics and genres.

Below are portraits of these eleven girls that paint a picture of commonality, and also of difference. Each girl has a distinct voice, and yet each is tied to each other through a common voice, a voice they share as pre-adolescent fifth-grade girls.

Introductory Portraits of Eleven Girls

The brief introductions of the eleven girls in Mr. Roscoe's fifth-grade classroom are presented here, mostly, through their own writing that reflect and reveal what these girls are like. Some of the girls' pieces I present are initial, rough drafts not intended to be revised, while others are more polished or final drafts, intended by the girls to be published. No text has been edited by me, although I sometimes have inserted conventional spellings or certain words in brackets for readability. The pieces were created within various writing contexts, and although not the focus here, the particular context of each text will be noted.

In addition to their writing, I talk about these girls' cultural and linguistic heritages here as a way to identify them. Of the eleven girls in Mr. Roscoe's classroom, Jane was the only Angla. Of the remaining ten girls, two of the girls were African-American, while the rest were of Latina descent: four were from or had parents from Puerto Rico and four were from or had parents from Mexico. All but two of the girls were ten years old; Lucy and Walinda were eleven years old. All of the girls who were of Latina descent were bilingual, at least orally.

This kind of description is problematic though, because it was never very helpful, nor descriptive to pigeonhole any one of these girls by her ethnicity or language. It was much easier to categorize them similarly by their gender and by their socioeconomic status, i.e., their poverty. It was in this way later that *they* too felt a camaraderie; a "we're all in this together" feeling, though I didn't hear from the girls about this common bond extensively until much later in the year.

In the beginning of the year, I learned other things about the girls in Mr. Roscoe's classroom. I begin with Jane.

Jane

Dear Mr. R.,

I am *10* years old. My birthdate is *November* 4 1981. My best book I like to read is Grils [girls] talke. My favrite T.V show is *Beverly* Hills 90210. The happiest time of my life was when my ant Barb came from Kntoky [Kentucky]. The saddest time of my life was when my ant Barb came whit out Bill. My favorite thing about school is *wring* [writing]. My Health Problem is Hearing Impaired. I warde [wear] Hearing adse [aids]. I warde tow of them. And I don't like them but I have to warde them so I can hear, but i dont have to warde them when I am in the house or outside but I don't want to wire it outside so I won't loes [lose] it when I am plaing. I like to ward it in school so I can heard. I like my new teacher He is nice Hes name is Mr. R., He can help me when I need help.

Sinerly, Jane

Jane, considered "hearing impaired" with "minimal language abilities" by the language and hearing pull-out teacher, wore two hearing aids concealed by her long, blonde hair. But Jane's disability did not prevent her in anyway from being an integral part of the social networks that formed among the eleven girls in Mr. Roscoe's classroom. In fact, Jane, a ten-year-old Angla, was at the center of these peer groups that formed such a tightly-knit classroom community. Jane did her work and kept fairly quiet. Both Mr. Roscoe and the other girls in the classroom seemed to like her. And yet, the above piece, written in her response journal early in the school year, reveals a certain sense of insecurity around her disability. Jane felt a deep need to explain this insecurity as a way to "let everyone know about my hearing."

Yolanda

Yolanda, with her long jet-black hair and ruffled dresses, often speaking Spanish to the other Latina girls in the classroom, was a wisp of a girl. She didn't begin to speak to me until two months into the school year. She always smiled at me politely, dipping her head and averting her eyes as she did, but she never spoke.

Yolanda, Mexican-American, I learned, kept great "secrets," as the school year and our ultimate friendship developed. One of those secrets she revealed to Mr. Roscoe early in the year in two separate response journal entries. It was a secret, I later understood, that shaped much of Yolanda's view of the world.

Dear Mr. Roscoe

I'am 10 years old. My birthday is november 22. I was born in Mexico. The best book I ever read was Love you for-ever. My favorite movie is Bingo, gostwriter. The hapies time of my life was when we went to the sears tower. The sadiest time of my life was when my little brother die. My favorite thing about school is that I learn somthig new every day. have a good day

Yolanda

Dear Mr. R.,

I just want to tell you that I am sad because my mother had a baby boy after me and the baby died because my mother was four months and the baby was born and he

died. then after him she had a girl and she died too,
because she was too little, and also because she worked
alot. then she had a girl again and she is 4 years old now
she had a girl she is 4 months (the baby)

Sincerely
Yolanda

Yolanda carried with her small frame and averted eyes,
a great sadness. At the age of ten she had seen two deaths in
her family, ones that her mother blamed herself for by saying that she had "worked too hard." Yolanda worked very
hard in school and at home, diligently pleasing all of those
around her.

Maribel

Maribel, whose family was originally from Puerto Rico,
was always trying to please those around her, especially the
older adult women with whom she had contact (including
female teachers and administrators, myself, and her
mother). Although I never saw her interact with her mother,
Maribel reported that her mother was a constant source of
information and support for her, teaching her among other
things how to act "like a lady." Maribel says she loved this
role, spending a lot of time asking me and others about
manners, makeup, and other so-called feminine necessities.
These necessities seemed to be especially important to her
as she actually perceived herself as a sickly, powerless girl.

Her writing often revealed these sickly images of herself and at the same time seemed to help her feel better,
both physically and emotionally. "The Day I Had My Tunsels
taken out in Surgery," written during writing workshop,
was a typical piece for Maribel.

In November, 11, 1991, I had surgery. It was a friday. I
went at 6:30 a.m, and I went to Hospital St. Elizabeth. I
went to the Recovery room to wait for the doctor to come.
He came at 9:35 a.m. to take me to the surgery room and
they put me to sleep with a shot. They did my surgery,
then they called my mother to come SEE me at the hospi-

tal, and I was in the recovery room w̶i̶a̶t̶i̶n̶g̶ ̶f̶o̶r̶ ̶m̶y̶ mother
and I was bleeding through, my mouth. I was like asleep,
like a dead person lien [lying] down on those beds, I was 2
beds, because they changed me! I was two days in that
hospital I thought I was going to died. The third day I
went home and I got out from the hospital. And when I got
home my father was working and he came to the house I
was sleeping and he gave me a kiss and a big hug and
$10.00 and went to sleep with my mom.

Maribel was later hospitalized for anemia and then for
some sort of an "infection" during the school year. Through
her illnesses, though, she seemed to gather strength and
knowledge about sickness and disease. Maribel was a prolific writer always searching for opinions on her writing
(from me, her peers, and Mr. Roscoe) or more information to
put into her pieces.

Nayda

Nayda, also from Puerto Rico, tried to please others as
well, struggling most with trying to please her father. Her
father had left years ago and had moved to Indiana. She
had only seen her father once during the five or so years
that he had been gone. Nayda seemed to be obsessed over
her father. She blamed herself for his leaving and she spent
a lot of time in her writing finding a way to alleviate the
pain over losing him.

Nayda wrote draft after draft of *My 1st Time Going To
Indiana* in writing workshop, a semi-fictional account of
the only time she was permitted to visit her father.

My 1st Time Going To Indiana

When I was 4 years old my Dad, Nick took me to Indiana
for the first time. I asked my Mom if she wanted to go
she said, "No." So, I went to Indiana. Then my Dad took
me to a store called Frank's and I got lost. Then I couldn't
find my Dad. I went around the whole store and I found
my Dad and he said, "where have you been, I was looking
all over the store." So my Dad took me in the car and he

went back in the store to finish buying what he had to buy. When my dad left, I started to play in the car. I was messing with the shifting gear and when I stopped playing with the gear, I noticed that the car was moving. Then I jumped out of the car and I broke my ankle. The car kept on moving and it crashed into the store. Then it blew up and all the people from the store ran out. When my Dad Nick came out, he was mad. His face was cherry red, his eyes looked like they were going to pop out. I was going to run, but I couldn't beacause I broke my ankle. So I stayed where I was sitting. Then I told my dad that when I jumped out of the car I broke my ankle. My Dad picked me up and walked me to the doctor and the doctor told me that I have to wear a cast for two weeks. After we came from the doctor's I went home. My dad took me to my house and my mom, Carin, saw the cast and started fighting with my Dad. My mom threw my dad out of the house and I never saw my dad ever agian. THE END.

Nayda insisted that "most" of the events of this story about her father were true, especially the part about her parents fighting. When nudged by me, however, she did admit that the car running into the store and the store blowing up was fictional, but that she put that "stuff in there so it would be more exciting." As of this draft of "My 1st Time Going to Indiana," Nayda had still not seen her father again. Yet he remained the focus of much of her life and she and I had numerous conversations about "alternative" families, fathers, and children.

Laurelei

Laurelei, Mexican-American, who took a bus for an hour to remain at Near-Northwest Elementary school, was the only girl who regularly participated in large group writing workshop activities such as Author's Chair (see chapter 1). But she did not do this as a way to please others, as some of the other girls might have done. Laurelei was overweight and for this reason was constantly picked on by the boys in the class. Perhaps because of this teasing, she asserted herself in public ways that others did not. Yet it was unheard of for Laurelei to write on ~~topics that directly~~ revealed anything about her personal life or herself.

It was hard to get to know Laurelei and early on I suspected that her tough exterior was hiding a vulnerable, hurt girl. Indeed, as the school year progressed, Laurelei became increasingly quiet and withdrawn. She was easily hurt and it was not uncommon in conversations I had with her for her to cry, asking me why people were so cruel.

In the following excerpts of a tape-recorded conversation Laurelei and I had late in the school year about why she wrote, she talked about her perceived persecution and how writing helped "a little."

BRETT: Do you think writing helps you to talk about personal things in your life?

LAURELEI: Yeah, a little bit . . .

BRETT: 'Cause I know you wrote some letters to Mr. R., like I don't think you would have said it to him.

LAURELEI: Yeah like remember the letter I wrote to him? I lost it.

BRETT: Yeah, I know. So you wouldn't have ever said that, you wrote it down.

LAURELEI: Yeah because I wrote it up, because if I said it, I wouldn't be able to said it. I wouldn't be able to say, just like face-to-face.

BRETT: Do you like Near-Northwest school?

LAURELEI: Do you want me to tell the truth?

BRETT: Yes, I want you to tell the truth.

LAURELEI: Because I don't like to be in that room.

BRETT: Why?

LAURELEI: I dunno. Anyways I don't like Mr. R., he's not there when people hit me or anything. I just don't like him.

Laurelei's self-esteem seemed to suffer greatly from the constant ridicule she was subject to. Further, she never understood why Mr. Roscoe (who, in fact, intervened on her behalf often) was not a bigger advocate for her.

Lucy

Lucy was quite the opposite from Laurelei. A very popular girl, she came from a very strict religious Puerto Rican background. I had learned this one day early in the year when, on our way to lunch, I noticed she carried a lunch box and asked her why. (I knew that every student in Mr. Roscoe's classroom qualified for the state subsidized lunch.) She replied that because of her family's beliefs, there simply was some food she couldn't eat. "Lots of people think it's cause I got sick on the food once, but that's not why," she added.

Lucy was the only girl in the class who seemed to move freely within the boys' circles, laughing and hitting them as if they were her best friends. She talked most often about her friends, male and female, connecting herself to them through her stories. The following short piece she wrote early in the year in writing workshop highlights her sense of connection to Walinda, the only other eleven-year-old girl in the classroom.

Me and Walinda

Walinda is tall, funny, crazy, she has short brown hair, brown eyes, and also smart. I am tall, funny, crazy, I have long brown hair and brown eye, and smart. We play, talk, run, ring doorbells every day after school. Once Walinda knoted a bathroom window a guy came naked we ran the fastest we could. She sometimes comes by My house or I'll go by her house.

Walinda

Lucy's best friend, Walinda, the only other eleven-year-old, and one of two African American girls in the classroom was the first girl to actively befriend me. I can remember clearly the first day I met Walinda. She wore baggy jeans with a purple sweatshirt draped around the multi-colored tee shirt she wore. Her hair was braided and she wore bright purple and red beads in her hair that made noise when she walked or flipped her bangs out of her face. Her bangs were always in her face. Walinda spent a lot of time watching me sitting in the back of the room. She always smiled when I caught her eye. Walinda had a terrific smile; genuine and bright. I didn't know it at the time, but Walinda would become what anthropologists in the field traditionally call a "primary informant" (Spradley 1980). Walinda kept me informed on all levels about a lot of things. When I didn't understand something that was going on in the classroom, I often went to Walinda. Mr. Roscoe saw Walinda as a student who never finished her work. I saw Walinda as a young woman who had a lot of work to do.

Walinda had a lot of work to do when she left school each day to go home. Both Walinda's mother and older siblings worked at night, leaving her alone to do the daily cooking and cleaning. The role was so demanding (but well-paying she told me) that she was literally alone, not able to find the time to visit with friends or do her homework. Consequently, she relied on the phone and television for companionship.

> I am all alone at home and I am scary and staring at the pone [phone] I wait and want some more and no one calls it it is such a bore. I clan [clean] the house and I saw [sew] and cook and thin [then] I think I call my frinds my pal my budy to the pone. I grap [grab] the pone no longing [longer] blue and I love and talk with you.

I worried that Walinda would soon drop out of school altogether. But I knew, too, that school was really one place that Walinda was able to socialize, and I hoped that that aspect of schooling alone could keep her interest so that she would remain.

Chantal

Chantal was the second African-American girl in the classroom. She was a prolific writer whose pieces often mirrored her playful, teasing personality. She often wrote about her family and extended family members, taking ideas from books she read or from actual events she witnessed like her baby brother peeing all over the floor, or her grandmother and aunt who cursed at each other. And yet, Chantal also could be a serious writer and in the following piece, details for her audience her perceived future.

> When I grow up
>
> When I grow up I will finish school. I will work at Mc'Donalds. When I get my pay check I will by me a house. before I get marry. I will buy a car and I will be driving it all day long. Then I will get marry and go on a honeymoon. Then I will have a baby. Her name will be Alexzandra. My husband will be working until my baby be going to school Then I be working at Mc'Donald's.

The many funny stories Chantal wrote served to hide a serious young woman, a young woman who seemed to be hiding a much more serious side to her personality.

Cynthia, Teresa, and Alejandra

Cynthia, Teresa, and Alejandra (along with Yolanda who I have already introduced) participated in a two hour long "bilingual extension" pull-out program every day. The program was voluntary (the girls' parents enrolled them) and was intended to help those students recently transitioned into "mainstream" classes to maintain their native language. The program, however, served to separate these four girls from the rest of the classroom, a fact that even the girls complained about. They were rarely present for writing workshop, for example, and as a result lost the experiences of community-building and collaboration around writing that Mr. Roscoe created for his students. Thus, these girls were not only physically but also emotionally isolated from the rest of the class. They produced few written pieces and literally huddled together in the back of the room to speak Spanish among themselves whenever they got the chance. Samples of pieces written in the beginning of the year (as a response to a prompt by Mr. Roscoe about what each student would like to be when she/he grew up) showed that meeting others' needs was prominent in their lives.

Cynthia, Mexican-American and like some of the other girls in the classroom, was the eldest female sibling in the family. Consequently she took on many domestic duties in the family, as this piece reflects.

> One day I was cooking Rice for my little sister and brother. that time my mother was weith her friend to help her fix the car and tack [take] care of the baby. So my brothers and sister was hongri [hungry] so I cook for them. I cook rice with meat and beans.

Although proud, initially, of her abilities to manage an entire household alone, later in the year Cynthia expressed through her public writing a great sense of trepidation over the responsibilities she was expected to assume.

> The day I stay with my sister
>
> it was sunday the 9 of dicember my mom let my [me] stay [but] I have to wath [watch] my sister and take care of it and when my mom wend [went] my little sister started crying and I give her milk and she did not whant some. I cary her and she still were crying. I change her diper and she still where crying and I play with her and she still were crying. I take her for a walk and she still were craying so we whent back to our house and she still where crying. I take her a Bath and she still were crying. my mom come at that moment and she stop crying when she heir [hear] the door and went. my mom come inside my mom hug her and she stop crying. I think she nide [need] her momy.

Further discussions in writers' workshop later in the year gave Cynthia support in her understanding of these demanding, and often frightening, roles.

Teresa, a very serious student, spent much of her time working quietly alone. Of Mexican-American heritage like the other girls in the bilingual program, Teresa often wrote about wanting to be connected to others and saw the field of nursing as one powerful way she could accomplish this.

When I grow up I want to achieve a cereer as a nurse. I
want to be a nurse because I could help sick people. When
you get your first pay check you could buy a house if you
save your money I would save a lot of money so I could get
a car. I would take my family. I will support to have 2 kid
and good husband. I will send my mother money for rent
and other stuff. If my mother don't have a car I will give
her a ride when she don't know how to drive. My family
would live happply [ever after].

For Teresa, being a nurse and caring for both strangers and
her family would lead to her family living happily ever after.
  Alejandra, Teresa's close friend also wrote about wanting to become a nurse. Like Teresa, Alejandra believed that
such a career would give her a better life, a "wonderful" life.

When I grow up I want to be a Nurse so I could help them
feel better. I like to be a nurse because you could give
shots to people. In the hospital you have stay up and you
don't get no sleep. In the hospital you have to write a lot of
stuff to give to the paingent [patient]. I like when we take
a break and do all you want. In the hospital sometime
the Nurse get of woke [gets awakened]. I want to be a
nurse because I to a wondful life [I too want a wonderful
life].

Teresa's and Alejandra's future aspirations mirrored
those of most of the other Latina girls in the classroom.
Nayda, Laurelei, Yolanda, Cynthia, and Maribel wanted to
enter traditionally female-dominated (and lower paying)
fields and become secretaries when they "grew up." Lucy
was the only Latina member of the group who wanted to
enter what she perceived to be a male-dominated field, that
of lab technician.

Summary

Various writing contexts were provided for the eleven
girls in Mr. Roscoe's classroom. Mr.

Roscoe's implementation of a writing process approach provided several of these contexts, including writing workshop, response journals, and letter writing. In addition, the context I developed, writers' circle, as a result of watching girls in previous classes become silent altogether, provided these eleven girls with a major avenue in which they could write and talk about what they wished.

The girls' writing presented here was created both in public and private contexts during the beginning of the school year and each girl chose to describe herself in different ways. For example, Jane wanted to let us know about her hearing impairment and could not even talk about herself without making reference to her hearing aids. Chantal, playful and funny in most of her public writing, showed a more serious side when asked to write about herself. Walinda and Lucy, the two eldest girls in the classroom, wrote and talked a lot in terms of each other. Maribel and Yolanda revealed despair and sickness. Laurelei reflected on her perceived victimization. And Teresa, Alejandra, and Cynthia did very little writing during Mr. Roscoe's classroom. Despite a discontinuity between their bilingual pull-out classes and Mr. Roscoe's writing workshop, these girls managed to stay connected to each other and others through expressing a common desire to enter into "caring" fields.

These introductory portraits of these eleven girls paint a picture of commonality, and of difference. Each girl has a distinct personality and voice, and yet each is tied to one another in many ways. The Latinas are tied to each other through a common native language; Lucy and Walinda by their ages; others by the fact that they lived in single-parent homes. And yet, it was perhaps the underlying theme of gender (in a classroom overrun with boys) blended with unmistakable poverty that was the one unifying theme that connected them to each other; the one paintstroke that when mixed together revealed a picture of hope, despair, struggle, and joy.

In the remaining chapters of this book, the girls' distinct and common multiple voices will become clearer as they are revealed in more detail through both the public and private contexts in which they wrote.

5

Public Writing Contexts I:
Expository and Non-fiction

In institutions of learning most [of these] women attended, the subjective voice was largely ignored; feelings and intuitions were banished to the realm of the personal and private. It was the public, rational, analytical voice that received the institutions' tutelage, respect, and rewards. (Belenky et al. 1986, p. 124)

Learning to express one's voice, both publicly and privately through writing, entails learning to struggle and sort out a multitude of competing voices (Bakhtin 1981, 1986). For girls, this struggle becomes a process of articulating voices that may be at the same time, "emotional, sexual, domestic, and at the margin" (Kehde 1991, p. 25), voices that are often banned to the "realm of the personal and private."

In this chapter, the public voices that the eleven girls in Mr. Roscoe's classroom shared through non-fiction writing such as expository writing will be explored. It is important to look at the girls' voices here through non-fiction (and in the next chapter through fiction and narrative) because of the different, multiple voices that were heard. These voices were not only different because of the genres the girls used through which to write, but also because of the genres of texts that frequently influenced their writing.

Reading-Writing Connections:
Expository and Other Non-Fiction

Recently, there has been research on the issue of whether narrative should be seen as primary in literacy development (Bruner 1986; Langer 1985; Newkirk 1987; Pappas 1993a, 1993b). This research has been quite important for a discussion not only about the genres that students should be able to read and understand but also about the genres students should be able to attempt to produce in writing. Far little research, however, has focused on the development and expression of voice through genres other than narrative. These genres include non-story forms such as exposition, autobiography, and persuasion.

Typically, it has been thought that voice is frequently altogether squelched in non-story genres as students "grudgingly make the transition [from narrative to exposition for example] but the voice in their writing doesn't survive" (Fletcher 1993, p. 76). Non-fiction genres are perceived as more restrictive and less able to allow the writer to express his/her voice (Lensmire 1994).

In Mr. Roscoe's classroom, different genres represented different purposes, and therefore elicited different voices. Although he spent a lot of time modeling what these purposes might entail (e.g., poetry to a parent, persuasive essay to the President), the girls constantly complained that these non-fiction genres did not allow them to write about what they wished (boys and families, for example) thereby expressing the voices they wished. Nevertheless, they produced a number of non-fiction pieces often modeled after the books they were reading.

Mr. Roscoe made great efforts in making this connection between reading and writing explicit to his students. For example, he implemented a *readers'* workshop into his curriculum, setting aside most of the afternoon for reading "activities," including teacher read-aloud, guided reading, silent reading, reader response, and completing reader logs. In addition, many of his thematic units included strong science and social studies components and therefore integrated the use of a wide variety of appropriate non-fiction literature. Mr. Roscoe encouraged his students to make connections between and within content areas as they experimented with topics, genre, and voice.

Reading and writing are inherently connected and
readers of any discourse become its writers as they reconstruct and express meanings (and voices) of a text. That is,
there is a "complicity" of readers and writers in all acts of
composing and creating meaning through and by texts
(Crowley 1989, xii). What this means in the classroom is
that writing and reading are not necessarily merely related,
but are aspects of the same activity. Singh (1989) expresses
the activity this way:

> This [happens] not merely because we learn to write by
> imitating models; rather, all discourse is discourse on dis-
> course, all writing about writing, and therefore writing is
> not possible unless it is preceded by, goes simultaneously
> with, and results in, the reading of other writing . . . or
> what Bakhtin has chosen to see as [writing's] dialogic
> nature. (p. 168)

In the following section I present samples from the
girls' repertoire of non-fiction pieces which served an important function for the girls' expressions of a range of public
voices in the classroom.

Heroes, Space, and Alligators

Laurelei was one of the girls who truly loved to write
biographies. Her biographies were especially interesting to
others as she usually wrote them on fairly obscure public
figures whose lives and accomplishments were not necessarily well-known. The following "bio" on Harry Houdini is
one example.

Bio:
Harry Houdini

Harry Houdini was Born in, Budapest, Hungary, on
March 24, 1874. Houdini's real name is Ehrich Weiss. One
day Harry's father killed a man it was of Busines
Problems and they forced him to move with his family to

Appleton, Winsconsin. When Harry was Fourteen, his family mved again to New York hoping for Better opportunities there. One time Harry needed work badly and he found some people in line for a work as a nectie cutter and then he played a trik on all of Them by saying that somebody took the job allready, and then he wen't in the office and claim it for himself. For the next two and a half years he spend his days as a necktie cutter and evenings reading and practicing simple tricks. One of the Books he was reading was on the french magician 'Robert Houdin.' a friend told Harry to add an 'i' to the word Houdin so it would be Houdini. At age seventeen he felt he was ready for a career in magic he quit his job and formed an act called "The Brothers Houdini" His first partner was from his tie cutting days. Later his younger Brother theo took over, they performed were ever [wherever] audience was.

In this piece Laurelei reports on details of Houdini's life that she found important and amusing. Retelling (to me in a private discussion) how the story was received in Author's Chair, Laurelei recalled both the laughter over Houdini's "trick" in the factory line and the interest by many of the boys in performing like-tricks. Perhaps because this piece was so well-received, Laurelei spent a lot of time creating similar biographical stories on a range of lesser-known, not-so-popular heroes such as Sally Ride and Teddy Roosevelt.

Chantal and Jane also liked to write biographies. In the following co-authored text, Chantal and Jane describe Martin Luther King's early life and his meeting on Rosa Park's behalf.

Martin Luther King

Martin Luther King JR. was born in Atlanta, Georgia, on January 15, 1929. Martin got married to Coretta and they had 4 kids: two boys and two girls. During the time of Martin, Black people could not sit in front of the bus. They could not even eat in public.

One day Mrs. Rosa Parks got on a bus in Montgomery, Alabama. She was very tired and a white man wanted

her seat in the front of the bus. She said, "No!" So the
police took her to jail.

Martin became a minister instead of a fireman which was
his boyhood dream. He finished high school when he was
15 years old. Martin studied to be a Doctor of Religion.
So he was called Dr. Martin Luther King Jr.

Martin had a meeting about Rosa's problem. They decided
that they would fight about it. Martin didn't believe in
violence. He was different from the others.

Martin never got to finish his fight. One day, Martin died
because of a man who did not believe in his dream.

Chantal and Jane's retelling of Dr. King's life is punc-
tuated with profound senses of injustice and inequity.
Discussions we had (in writers' circle and other conversations about drafts of this piece) around such statements like
"he was different from the others" and he "died because a
man who did not believe in his dream" (lines I picked out
and asked the girls specifically to talk about) showed how
Chantal and Jane were beginning to make sense of racism,
for example. One way they did this was to talk publicly
about their friendship, using their solid working relationship as a model to others on how important accomplishing
things together was.

A lot of the other non-fiction pieces that the girls created included expository writing around the thematic unit of
THE SOLAR SYSTEM. Most of the eleven girls complained
that this writing was "boring" but their pieces were usually
not really boring at all and often revealed subtle expressions of their voices.

For example, Teresa's piece on "Jupiter" was quite typical of the kind most of the girls created for THE SOLAR
SYSTEM thematic unit.

Jupiter

Jupiter is called the King of the Giants because it is the
biggest planent in the solar system. Jupiter is so big that
it can fit more than 1,300 Earth's in it because it is so big

that it could fit all that Earth's in it. If you weight 85
pounds on Earth in Jupiter you could weight 245 pounds.
In Earth you weight less than on Jupiter because Jupiter
has more gas than on Earth. Jupiter started first with
four moons. Then in a will [while] they slip up and be
come 16 moons and that's how Jupiter had 16 moons.

Teresa's paraphrasing of books she read in her inquiry
about Jupiter helped her to sort out new and difficult content area information such as "weightlessness" and "gravity." Sorting out information through writing was an important strategy for many of the girls as they were able to learn
new concepts while they practiced writing genres not so
familiar to them. This, then, at the same time afforded them
opportunities to experiment with voices that weren't so
familiar.

For example, some of the girls expressed enthusiastic,
excited kinds of voices through their non-fiction pieces and
expressed great surprise to find themselves able to do this.
In the following piece on the sun, Alejandra expresses her
great fascination of the sun through a visually exciting
piece.

The Sun

The sun is a star. The Sun's energy keeps every thing on
earth alive. The sun's energy lifts the water out of the
oceans and makes the rain. The sun's enery makes hurricanes and rainbows. The solar system is the Sun and all
it's planets.

The sun may be just a star in the universe but in the
Solar System it's giant. More than a hundred earths culd
fit side by side across the sun. The sun is a huge and flam-
ming ball of gas. Deep inside the sun the temperature is
millions of degrees hot. Hydrogen is the fuel that keeps
the sun burning. Hydrogen is a gas.

It would take 1,3000,000 earth's to make a ball as large as
the sun. The Earth's distance is 93 million miles. Inside
the sun is a core twice as big as Jupiter, that core is like
27 million degrees hot!

Sometimes there are huge explosions on the sun. The sun
looks like it has freckles. But they are called sunpots.
some of the sunpots are bigger than the Earth. Sunpots
are special types of electrical storm. Sunpots can effect
the weather on Earth.

Like in eleven years the sunpots start growing up.

The shinning surface of the sun is a sea of boilling gases.
When the moon covers the sun completely it's called total
eclipse. The moon is much closer to us than the sun is.
Scientists think that the sun began as a enormous cloud of
gas and dust. Like over a billions years ago, the matter in
the cloud came together. Then the cloud got hotter. Then
about 4 1/2 billion years ago it got so hot it began to burn.
There is enough fuel in the sun to keep it going for
another 5 million years. As it's fuel is used up, the sun
will turn into a red giant star. The End.

Alejandra's enthusiasm of the topic is expressed clearly
and highlighted by her choice of phrases to describe the sun
(the sun looks like it has freckles), imagery (the shining
surface of the sun is a sea of boiling gases) and exclama-
tion points. Alejandra was, indeed, surprised, she said, lean-
ing over me one day as I typed this story for her to display
on a hallway bulletin board, that she actually could get
excited about something as "boring" as the sun.

Maribel's piece on alligators reflects this sense of excitement around finding and expressing "new" multiple voices
through experimentation with different genres. Although
heavily modeled after a Shel Silverstein poem (Maribel
"thought" that's where she got the idea and I was unable to
locate any direct source) the following text (for those who
know her) clearly mirrors Maribel's personality and
demeanor.

Never Kiss an Alligator!

Never kiss an alligator, hug, an alligator, pat, poke, push,
hit, kick or even touch an alligator, because alligators bite!
When you meet an alligator usually at a zoo, what should
you do? Whatch, look and learn, for alligators are fasanat-

ing! Alligators are ancient, and lived when the dinosaurs lived about two hundred million years ago. The name alligator is from a Spanish word "el lagarto" which means the lizard. Lizards do look like miniature alligators. Alligators are found in only two parts of the world: a few in eastern China, most in the warm southeastern United States especially Louisiana and Florida. Alligators live in water beside water half in and half out of water. They stay in ponds beside an algae-covered pond in swaps [swamps], marshes, lakes, rivers, streams, and somethimes in people's swiming pools, fish ponds and in water or golf courses.

As the school year progressed, some of the girls including Maribel became much bigger fans of non-fiction genres, experimenting more widely both with the genres themselves and the newly expressed voices they heard as a result of their experimentation.

Explanations and Regrets

In this final section of the chapter, I present samples of the girls' apology note and letter writing. Although not sanctioned necessarily as an "official" component of the writing workshop, apology notes and letters became a de facto part of the workshop in Mr. Roscoe's classroom. As a result, they represented opportunities in which the girls could express additional public voices.

The class as a whole wrote numerous notes throughout the year apologizing to lunchroom attendants, substitute teachers, the principal, other classroom teachers, and even to me. It was mostly the boys who wrote these notes (as they were usually the ones "in trouble") although on occasion (and always toward the end of the year) the entire class was asked to do so as well.

The girls' apology notes took on a persuasive style. The girls usually were not to blame for the incidents that led up to their writing of these notes and they resented having to explain, time after time, what had happened, to whom and by whom. And yet, they did so quite convincingly. They also became quite adept at exonerating themselves from any blame, using such strategies as "it wasn't that bad," "boys just don't know what they're doing," and "I'm not really sure what happened." (In contrast, most of the boys usually said things like, "I didn't do anything wrong," "nothing happened," or "it was so-n-so's fault.")

The persuasive style that the girls learned to express, voices of confusion and or regret, for example, were not modeled for them from books they were reading. Rather, Mr. Roscoe modeled this genre directly for his students. He often told them what he would like them to say (e.g., I'm sorry and next time I will . . .) and by the end of the year, the girls in particular had developed and internalized their own set of "rules" around how this writing should look. For example, the girls knew that these notes should always include a salutation, a few sentences explaining what happened, to whom and by whom, and a few final sentences on either what should have transpired or how the incident might look better another time.

The apology notes and letters were never shared in a large public forum like Author's Chair, but Mr. Roscoe would, on occasion, pick out a handful of notes to read aloud. It was in this way that he accomplished and established the public nature of these notes and rather explicit rules for their creation.

Although it occurred at the end of the year, a particularly disruptive incident in science class was typical to stimulate apology notes and on this day Mr. Roscoe demanded that the entire class write apology letters to the science teacher. The girls were particularly interested in clearing their names as the "punishment" for the disruption was losing their outdoor recess time. Maribel explained what happened this way:

Dear, Mr. Roscoe

Ms. M. [science teacher] was upset because people were talking standing up, and not pay attention. She recomend us not go outside for recess because of our disobidient behavior.

For Maribel, "people" did not include herself even though at the end of this short note she apologizes for "our" disobedient behavior. Her voice reflected her obedient behavior, a tactic she knew could only help persuade Mr. Roscoe to let them go outside for recess.

Jane took a different tack on the same incident, questioning the science teacher's story altogether. Rather than expressing obedience, perhaps, by admitting that "people" were indeed talking, Jane, through her writing, hints that the accusations made by the science teacher were not even necessarily true.

> Today in the Science Room Yolanda was talking and I was talking a little but then I stop and sarted [started] to write? becuse we all were runing arond and talking? And then we lined up and people was talking again But not a lot?

Jane's use of question marks literally punctuates this short note with a questioning, even challenging voice.

Cynthia, on the other hand, tries to dismiss the entire issue by attempting to persuade Mr. Roscoe (and herself) that it really wasn't that "bad." Cynthia was proud, she told me, that at least she "told the truth." A voice of honesty attempts to persuade Mr. Roscoe of the veracity of her statements.

> Today at Science it was not that Bad but some of the people were talking. Horace was not looking at the boart [board] un till the teacher toll [told] hem more than two times. Maribel the teacher had to caneng [continue] to ask because Maribel was talking to much with Lucy and Yolanda too. She toll you that if she was you that she would not take us out because most of the people were not listen to her thats why and because some people were playing and talking alot. Sincerely, Cynthia

Cynthia, as had many of the other girls, became immune to the fighting and violence around them, a topic discussed in more detail in chapter 7 of this book. There, as in Cynthia's note above, voices of rationalization and dismissal were evident.

In apology notes Mr. Roscoe had the class write to me one day after four fights had erupted among the boys (again toward the end of the year), the girls voices were extremely regretful. I cried when I read the notes, knowing as the girls did that they were not involved in the fighting whatsoever.

For example, Jane attempted to persuade me that it's the heat that makes the boys fight. And just in case she might have done something wrong, she asks for my forgiveness.

> Dear Brett
>
> I am sorry and what happen in this room. It is just hot in herar when it get hot it get trouple [trouble] I am sorry I did anything. I hope you cold [could] forgive some of us. And thanks fro trying to solve my proplems.
>
> Jane
>
> Have a nex [nice] summer. I no [know] I wont.

Jane, too, begins to rationalize the violence in the classroom, as she attempts to explain it away by blaming the incidents on the hot weather.

Nayda, on the other hand, tries to convince me that she and the whole class is simply "bad," hoping such a blanket explanation would satisfy me.

> Dear Brett,
>
> I am sorry for what hapend today. I know we were a very very bad class. When you come again (if you do) we won't be this bad agian. Sincerly, Nayda

And Lucy assumes that her classmates' lack of respect will make me leave the classroom and never come back. In her note, she tries to let me know how important I was to her.

> Dear Brett
>
> I very sorry of my classmates respakte [respect]. I do know [not know] how to speell that word. I really hope I can

see you next year but I Don't blame you. I would'nt want to come next year either if I were [you] and it [it's] your last day. I'm going to miss you if I want to a lady who's not my mom and tell you like a little bet stuff [a little bit of stuff]. But I'm really really going to miss you. Sincerely, Lucy

Finally, in her letter, Alejandra asks me to "forgive" *the boys* that were involved, attempting to convince me both through this note and a subsequent conversation that boys just don't know what they're doing.

Dear. Brett

I am sorry than things are happing [happening] with boys and about boys where [were] not writeing and thouing [throwing] paper asept [except] Roberto. Roberto was the one who was doing a story and some of the girls sorry and forgive this boy that wasen't behaveing good we love you and others teachers. Sincerely, your friend you can all- ways cout [count] on it. Alejandra p.s. sorry and I hope you don't get mad we [with] me

Alejandra's explanation about why boys disrupted every- thing seemed to be the ultimate rationalization for behavior that the girls had begun to accept as routine.

Writing apology notes was for the girls an extremely important avenue in which they could through persuasion and exposition, and therefore express additional voices. Although intended for public use, the girls adapted the rules of how these notes should look and included their own expressions and versions of what had happened. These notes, then, often took on a private, personal tone, as the girls expressed their own voices saying such things as "I'm sorry" and "Forgive us."

Although not made explicit through the books they were reading, but rather by Mr. Roscoe, this non-fiction genre seemed to help the eleven girls in Mr. Roscoe's class- room to begin to develop senses of writing for public audi- ences in often very private ways.

Summary

When asked, the eleven girls in Mr. Roscoe's classroom would say that non-story genres were clearly not their preferred genre. They did however experiment with biography and exposition and this experimentation afforded them opportunities in which to express their particular, multiple voices.

In this chapter, I have focused on the public voices that the girls expressed through non-fiction genres such as biography, exposition, and persuasion. These non-fiction genres produced a myriad of voices from the girls, influenced directly by either the books they read or the writing Mr. Roscoe modeled for them. Multiple voices of humor, concern, confidence, enthusiasm, blame, confusion, and regret were revealed.

In the following chapter, the public voices that the girls expressed through fiction and narrative, revealing additional, various voices will be explored.

6

Public Writing Contexts II:
Narrative and Fiction

> The sets of cultural knowledge that children use in their
> writing are not homogeneous but diverse and full of con-
> tradictions . . . girls' stories for evidence of struggle—
> struggle to deal with dominant versions of masculinity
> and femininity, and struggle to find space within the con-
> ventions of popular fiction to write differently and more
> powerfully. (Gilbert & Taylor 1991, p. 110)

Lensmire (1994) describes the writing workshop as a riskier place for some students than others. In Mr. Roscoe's classroom, the writing workshop as a public forum for students' writing was indeed a vulnerable place for the girls to express their voices. This was apparent for two interrelated reasons.

First, the boys outnumbered the girls by an almost 3 to 1 ratio, rendering the girls' struggles for their voices to be heard even more intense. Second, many of the issues that the girls wished to write about in their personal narratives were not well received by the male members of the classroom. That is, the boys frequently made fun of, laughed, or simply dismissed the girls when they talked about their families or the birth of a sibling.

In this chapter I share some of the girls' narrative and fictional pieces created within the public context of writing workshop, highlighting the influences on their voices from literature and their daily lives. Additional foci are the struggles they encountered in finding voices of their own and finding ways to feel that these voices were valued enough to be shared in public in the classroom. First, however, I turn to another (see previous chapter) brief explanation of reading/writing connections, with two samples from the girls' writing, and their relationship to voice through fiction and narrative.

Reading-Writing Connections: Fiction and Narrative

It seemed that the girls' reading of "formulaic" litera- ture, i.e., literature that presented girls and women, and others, in traditional, stereotypic ways influenced their nar- rative and fictional writing. According to feminist analyses of literary genres, this kind of stereotypic literature makes the transition and connection to writing troublesome for girls. In Gilbert's (1989) view, this occurs because most stories,

> typically show men dominating and controlling women's lives; show men as physical and aggressive, and women as passive and self-sacrificing; and show 'love' and 'romance' as the ultimate and optimum life-goals for women. (p. 262)

As a result girls have difficulty constructing stories from such formulaic models, potentially rendering girls' stories full of tensions and unresolved conflicts.

These formulaic frameworks not only affect how girls are perceived through literature, but how they perceive themselves and other women through their constructing of texts modeled after what they have read. These frameworks, then, in particular also affect the kinds of voices girls express in public ways.

Chantal, for example, created a Christmas story around a formulaic theme where good triumphs over evil; modeled after countless popular Christmas stories that Chantal had read and seen on television like "How the Grinch Stole Christmas."

The Christmas Party

It happend December the 25. The people was very happy in the village. One day a man came and he hated

Christmas. The man was very evil. The man always take happy people and make people intoo bad people they would Destroy the village until a strong man came and beet the bad people and take the bad people to his castle and make them happy. So in the little village the people had a happy Christmas party.

While the pattern after which Chantal modeled this piece is identifiable, the underlying tensions and the unresolved conflicts Chantal creates through this story are not so obvious. First, both main characters, evil and strong, are men. Bad people are turned to happy people, and everybody, in the end, has a happy Christmas. The male characters are controlling and are physically aggressive, while the ultimate goal is love and happiness. These story elements come directly from Chantal's exposure to literature (and television), and are particularly troublesome to her expression of voice.

Chantal, as an African-American girl, began to understand that there is little literature in school that helps her to make connections to her life. In fact, in a conversation with me about what she was reading one day she wanted to know why everything she read was about "white people" and "men." As a result of our conversation around this issue, I began to bring her other things to read, including pieces and short stories by Toni Cade Bambara. She became so interested in pieces written about and by African-Americans and women, that she requested that I read aloud to her "Raymond's Run" (1980) because it was too hard for her to read on her own. (When I reached the part where Mary Louise, Rosie, and Squeaky trade stories, Chantal exclaimed, "They talk just like me." At the end of the story when I asked, "Did you know Squeaky would win?" she responded with, "All the time, I'm faster than both my sisters and they're older." Finally, she asserted, "I'm gonna make me my own story like this.")

The formulaic books Chantal claims she had always read previous to the writing I had given her always ended happily, as did most of her stories. However, Chantal's real

Christmas was not to begin nor end happily, a fact I learned about in private notes to me and her peers saying how she was "very sad that my mother be telling us [she's] not buying us presents." This sort of tense reality can be examined through literature and the reproduction of literature through writing.

Cynthia, too, wrote stories which exhibited unresolved conflicts and tensions and struggles over voice. In her piece, "The day I went to a dance," Cynthia presents the escalating conflict between her and her mother as she approaches adolescence:

> The day I went to a dance
>
> It was March 8, 1993 it was Monday I whent with my sister and a friend of my sister he was a boy and his name was Joe his 11 year old his birthday is in April 8, and my birthday is in April 9, he is nice. he give me a teddy bear and we star[started] dancing and dancing every minutes. He star dancing with my sister and then we drink coconut with a little acohol and wene [when] I come home my mom see me good and she told me did you was drinking yes or no and I said I yest [just] drink alittle of acohol becuase it have coconut to and you now [know] I like coconut then she got mad with me and told me to tak a bath with cold water and I did then when I finish I call Yolanda and told her everything of the dance and then I whent to slepp and when I wake up my had [head] was hurting alot and my mom could not stop sceming [screaming].

Although on the surface this appears to be a story of a young woman going out, getting drunk with a boy, and getting yelled at by her mother, on closer analysis (and discussion with Cynthia), this piece reveals unresolved tensions around growing-up, being a girl, and developing relationships. However, because Cynthia has had no model from literature on which to begin to struggle with her own relationships in a strong, positive way, tensions in this piece are left unresolved. To illustrate her frustration, her mom's endless screaming becomes, perhaps, a metaphor for the screaming Cynthia feels in her own head.

The girls' fictional and narrative texts, although often based on formulaic patterns of male dominance and power, good and evil, and love and relationships, showed the unease with which these girls constructed these texts. The girls knew and understood that conflict and struggle was present in their lives, and yet, in their writing, could not often begin to resolve these struggles as they had little in the way of strong, positive models in literature on which to base their writing and to express their voices. In other words, there were no "alternative discourses" available to them; "no alternative discourses which offered them other ways of constructing the feminine" (Gilbert 1989, p. 263).

It was not uncommon for Mr. Roscoe to have to bring in books related to specific themes for his students, complaining that, it wasn't "easy to get good literature" for them, adding angrily one day, "Yea, did you know that RIF (Reading is Fundamental) dumps their non-sellers on these kids, you don't see any *good* literature here, like Judy Bloome, do you?". (There was a program where RIF gave away paperback books to any student who wanted one in the school). In addition, library funding, at best, was tenuous. For example, in May of the second year I was in Mr. Roscoe's classroom, he informed me that because of "budget cuts" the library would be closing *altogether*, two full months before the end of the school year. "How the hell can I expect to run a literature-based classroom?" he exclaimed when hearing of the news.

Most of the eleven girls in Mr. Roscoe's classroom were as prolific readers as they were writers, and what they wrote was modeled after what they read, so that the lack of available and quality literature had a major impact on the girls' expressions of their own voices through writing.

Babies, Bottles, and Boys

Other kinds of tensions and conflicts were revealed through the girls' construction of stories based on their daily lives. These struggles, although based in reality, still manifested themselves through the girls' fictional and narrative written texts. And these struggles, too, revealed unresolved tensions including those around an expression of voice. Primarily these tensions centered on finding voices that were valued in public forums.

In this section I present samples of the girls' written work that reflect "typical" pre-adolescent concerns including boys, families, new babies, and parties. These pre-adolescent concerns were most heavily influenced by the girls' daily lives, their families, and others' expectations and perceptions of them as pre-adolescents.

One theme that many of the girls wrote about was the sleepover, or slumber party, despite the fact that none of them had ever had a slumber party. Either their mothers worked at night, their houses or apartments were too small, or parents were simply too worried to take the girls out at night. And yet, desiring to be like the middle-class girls they had seen on television and in teen magazines, I was told, some of the girls spent a lot of time drafting stories about how a "real" slumber party might look like: full of antics, boys, and bedlam!

In the following piece by Laurelei we hear a wild tale of boys crashing a party. Here, according to Laurelei boys get just what they deserve, something, they never get when they "fool around" in the classroom.

THE GREAT SLUMBER PARTY

Once there was a girl named Judie. She was in 6th grade. She was 11 years Old. One day she decided that she was going to make a slumber party at her house and that it was going to be fun. She decided She was going to invite all her friends from school, except the boys, of course! It was going to be a girls slumber party. Any way, she called them. So, that friday night, all her frinds came. Later, they were playing lots of funny games. I don't Know how, but one of the boys Knew that we were having a slumber party, so that boy told the other boy's and they decided they were going to pick on us. It was so embarassing. They brought a ladder and climbed at my bedroom window. We were playing like we were movie stars. So we were moving like we

were big and we were dancing and waling and acting up.
When I turned around, I saw a boy at my bedroom window and I started yelling. Then all the girls Went to the
bedroom window and started hitting the boys in the head
with the pillows. Then, when my mom came, the boys got so
scared that they didn't know what to do. They Just stared
at my mom and all of a sudden, the ladder came down and
the boys went "Wooaaaa!" Lucky for them there was
another boy watchin he ladder, so the boys didn't hurt
themselves alot. The other boy, that was watching the ladder, made sure it didn't fall. When the ladder was about to
fall, the boy held it a little bit; then he let it go. They were
laying on the grass, they were complaining about themselves, then me and my mom looked out the window. They
looked up and started running. Three were in my class
room. One of them was the dum Jake and he was the one
watching the ladder. The other two were Miguel and Jaison.
In the morning, my mother and I went with Jaison's
mother, Miguel's mother, then with Jake's mother. And
guess what they all said! "You're grounded for two week's!"
And guess what, I said every time I left every single house?
"I am having another slumber party. Wanna come?"

Laurelei loved this piece so much that she had it typed for
her in the computer lab, published it, and put it into her
portfolio. A funny piece, it is interesting to note that
although she begins the story in the third person, she moves
to telling it in the first person. This change of person perhaps to reveals a hidden desire to be the girl in the story, the
girl who *can* have overnight slumber parties at her house.

Another typical interest of the eleven girls in Mr.
Roscoe's classroom was that of family members giving birth.
Since many of the girls' mothers, cousins, and older sisters
were at childbearing age, there were a lot of babies being
born. These events were a big deal among the extended
female family members and the girls retold the stories during the writing workshop.

Yolanda, the Mexican-American girl whose earlier writing described her mother's two miscarriages, finally had an
occasion to write about both her mother's good friend and
her mother having babies.

The day my mom had a baby

One day my mom's friend Elena was baby siting us and then
Elena was pragnett. My mom came from work. She noked
[knocked] on the door and elena opened the door it was my
mom. I ran to the door and huged her and then she sat down
and she started talking with elena about how many months
did she had. Elena said she had 3 and I think my mom said
that she had 1 month. So I said mom are you talking about
Elena and she said no I am pragnett too, I couldn't belive
her so when I went with her and the DR. told her that yes
she was prachnig [pregnant] then I belive it. Then when I
came to my house I told my mom to sit in the coach [couch]
and I did the dishes and mop the kitchen floor. Then my
father came and he did breakfast, lunch, and dinner. Then 5
months past by and she had 8 months and in november my
father told us that we were going to Mexico and we did.
When we came back from Mexico my mom was alredy going
to have the baby. And my aunt came in to live with us. and
when my mom was almost going to have the baby my aunt
said comon lets go to the hospital and my mom said "wait not
yet". we waited for 15 minutes and my aunt took my mom to
the hospital and they did not take me. then she had the Baby
then my uncle came to the house and he said do you wan't to
got the hospital I said "yes" he took me.

Then the nurse said to my mom what name do you want
to call the Baby and she said "Evelyn" the nurce put it in
a paper. Now she is 1 year old. She likes to see cartoons
and she does not wan't any garbage in the carpet!

Yolanda's voice resonates with excitement over her mom's
pregnancy, childbirth, and her family's involvement in these
events. The influences from a society that places great worth
onto pregnancy, childbirth, and connection by women has been
firmly ingrained into the voice Yolanda fashions in this piece.

Jane's voice reflects slightly different perspectives on
the same topic.

The day my baby cousin was born

My baby cousin was born on Dec 1 1992. We went to vist
him he was a baby boy his name was little Rickey. He

need to be changed so my ant Missy want to changed him
so she did but when she took of his daper off and he peed
all over her and he satard [started] laufing so hard that
every body on that floor started to laugh so she had to
take a rug and wipe him and her. She was full with wet
spots. so she put him in the bath tup and he splash water
all over her. And water got up his nose. When he got out
she dressed him and when she looked at him he started to
cry. And when she said what am I ugly And he stop crying.
And started to cry again. And she wen't on the porch and
he stop crying. Then we had to leve because we didn't eat
when we got home my ant Missy had to take a bath.
When she got out she thougt she seen him and then she
fell down. And then we put her to bed.

Jane's voice reveals an understanding of the hard work
that comes *after* a baby is born, expressing a reality that
some of the girls did not know existed even though they
either often cared for younger siblings or heard stories about
caring for younger siblings. This was made clear to me
increasingly through our writers' circle discussions around
sexuality and childbearing.

Specifically, through these discussions it became apparent that the voices the girls used in stories around pregnancy and childbirth were voices that reflected larger societal and cultural assumptions, e.g., childrearing is always
fun. The only voices many of the girls knew around these
topics were voices that reflected these assumptions—from
literature, from families, from school, from the media.
Further, because these particular texts were intended to be
shared in public, the girls did not make attempts to question
or challenge these assumptions in their texts. And finally,
although many of the girls in Mr. Roscoe's classroom were
privy to their female extended family members' conversations on pregnancy, childbirth, and childrearing most of the
girls were ill-informed about issues on their own sexuality,
including menstruation, conception, and birth control. (This
fact was disturbing considering that many of the girls had
begun their periods and had expressed interest in having
sexual relations with boys in the future.) As our writers'

circle meetings continued, however, many of these issues were addressed through private writing contexts. (See chapters 6 and 7.)

Trips to the Store and Trips Down the Stairs

Rather than risk writing publicly about some of the very personal issues mentioned above such as childbirth, the eleven girls developed strategies so that they could write fiction and personal narratives for public use. One of the strategies they used was to chronicle particular events or adventures of their family lives. In this way, the historical and cultural voices they knew best could be incorporated into their stories, while the topic of the story remained fairly neutral, non-controversial, even funny.

The multiple voices that the girls heard and understood best often came from their extended families, rendering in many cases their stories semi-autobiographical and biographical. In the following pieces, the girls write about events of their lives with their families.

Nayda spent a great deal of time writing about important events and adventures in her life. In the following excerpt of "My 1st Family Reunion," she describes what happened on this special day.

My 1st Family Reunion

My first family reunion happend on July 6, 1992. Me my brother, and my cousine went to Puerto Rico to practice our dance so we started practicin and on the next day we went to the reunion. Then I saw my aunt doing a really funny play it was about this one old lady who was trying to listen to her soap opera but she couldn't beacause her grandaughter had her radio volume up and she was dancing then she asked her grandmother if she wanted to dance with her so the grandmother said yes and she started to dance. And then the play finished. I thought the play was very funny beacause the grandmother was

moving her butt when she was dancing everybody liked
the play beacause the lady was the funny one in the play
beacause of the way she was dancing . . .

Nayda's piece on her family reunion was one that much
of the class (although Nayda never shared this in Author's
Chair, many of her peers read it or heard about it through
peer conferencing) found quite funny particularly about the
grandmother who was "moving her butt." Writing in a
humorous way was one important strategy the girls used
when writing for public audiences, emulating in many cases
the way certain boys in the class used humor to gain popu-
larity and respect.

Even pieces that were not intended to be funny were
better received, and thought by the girls to be "safer" if they
evoked laughter. Cynthia's narrative about the time her
mother fell down the stairs is one such example.

The Day my mom fell from the stairs with my stepfather.

He was laughing and my mother was crying and my step
father did not happen nothing [nothing happened to my
stepfather] and my mom did happen something I thing
[think] she fell becuase it was cold and the stairs was with
ice. I thing that her back star [started] hurt alot so she
when't to the dortor and the dortor said that noting was
wrong and she star tolding them it hurt

Cynthia shows quite clearly concern about her mother's
fall, but when she shared this piece, she reported that she
found her peers liked it because it was funny. She tended to
accept this peer response and shifted her voice from one of
concern to one of humor. Shifting one's voice (i.e., one's attitude toward a particular piece) to fit the needs of classmates
was a strategy many of the girls used in their writing.

Another tactic the girls used to create pieces that were
less risky to write and to share, was to write what I have
called "nondescript" stories. Nondescript pieces didn't evoke
laughter necessarily, but also didn't evoke any controversy

either. In this way the girls could produce pieces for public scrutiny without having to risk revealing much of themselves at all.

> When we saw our real grandmother
>
> It happend on Saturday morning. My mother pack us lunch and some pop. Then we left. We went to the train. We got of [off] at the end of stop we took the bus to Maywood. When we got there we ate. I went to sleep while my brother watch. my mother woke me up at 1:00 clock in the morning. When we got theere My Mother friend and his daughter they came in at 3:00 cloke [clock]. Then I woke up for a little and then I went back to sleep.

Here, Chantal simply lists events around one day of going to see her grandmother. Called "bed-to-bed" (Pappas, June 1994, personal communication) texts, these pieces are often seen as pieces devoid of any voice, a strategy, in the case of the eleven girls in Mr. Roscoe's classroom, that worked to allow them to share something noncontroversial in public arenas.

Summary

The models the girls were exposed to in the form of formulaic literature were not helpful in offering them alternative ways in which to write and express voices. In conversations I had with the girls about their writing and the books they read, the girls complained about (outside of personal experience) not knowing where to "get good stories from;" Chantal's question about why most of her reading involved white males seemed to support this issue. The girls clearly struggled over the multiple voices they heard from popular literature and their own voices that they wished to express.

In addition, the eleven girls clearly understood that certain voices and stories were more valued than others. That is, although they continued to write about typical female pre-adolescent concerns and about events in their lives through fiction and personal narrative, they adjusted their voices to better fit the dominant voices of the classroom, the male voices. In a very conscious way, the girls wrote on fairly safe and noncontroversial issues around things they knew. Topics such as sexuality were taboo (although a major focus of much of the boys' writing).

Genre choice was a crucial factor in determining how the girls fashioned their public voices. Different genres seemed to elicit different voices from the girls. Fiction or personal narrative put forth voices that were often familiar, revolving around families and boys, or safe and "nondescript", explaining events of a day. Non-fiction genres such as exposition and persuasion produced additional, often subtle voices, made explicit to the girls by Mr. Roscoe's modeling of particular genres and from the books they read on specific topics. And yet, throughout all the public writing activities the girls were exposed to, they continued to struggle with sorting out the multiple voices they heard and the multiple voices they knew, some their own, some that others wished to hear.

In the next chapter, I explore the girls' expression of voice through writing in contexts outside of the writing workshop. Specifically, the focus of this chapter is on the particular contexts made available for the girls to write in private and personal ways and three major themes that evolved from this personal writing. It was through these private, personal contexts that a great majority of the girls' writing was being created. It was also through these contexts that the girls began to fashion voices that were truly their own.

7

Private Writing Contexts I:
Domesticity, Family Life, and Sexuality

> Women hear themselves speaking in different voices in
> different situations. They hear themselves echoing the
> words of powerful others. And, like so many women, they
> feel like frauds. They yearn for a voice that is more inte-
> grated, individual, and original—a voice of their own.
> (Belenky et al. 1986, p. 124)

> For women within oppressed groups who have contained
> so many feelings—despair, rage, anguish—who do not
> speak, as poet Audre Lorde writes, "for fear our words
> will not be heard nor welcomed," coming to voice is an act
> of resistance. (hooks 1989, p. 12)

Private Writing Contexts and Audience

The eleven girls in Mr. Roscoe's classroom sought voices
of their own and through those voices resisted. Yet, these
voices were not necessarily apparent through public writing
contexts. In searching for voices of their own, a private, personal audience became the most powerful influence on not
only what the girls wrote but in what contexts, why, and
how.

Proponents of the writing workshop seldom consider
critically the effect audience has on shaping and constraining writing (Lensmire 1994, p. 140). In Mr. Roscoe's classroom, the writing workshop provided the largest public
audience in which students were eventually expected to

share their work. As I discussed in the previous two chapters, the girls not only rarely, if at all, participated in large group share-time activities, but also clearly modified what they wrote to their audiences.

There were, however, private contexts that Mr. Roscoe provided for all his students, plus the ones that I made available for the girls to write. (See chapter 4 for detailed descriptions of these contexts.) In this chapter the girls' private, riskful, and often resistant voices through various private writing contexts will be presented. These voices are revealed through three themes: domesticity, family life, and sexuality. These themes often intersected in the girls' writing and throughout their discussions around their writing and yet each theme represented a powerful set of separate issues that the girls desperately wanted to write and talk about.

Stories of Domesticity

Domesticity was a pervasive theme found throughout much of what the girls wrote and talked about as they began to see themselves as potential wives, childbearers, and homemakers. Although they wrote about the domestic roles others expected them to perform for writing workshop (see Cynthia's piece about cooking and Walinda's piece about being home alone in chapter 4), they also challenged and resisted certain views of domesticity with voices of resistance for more private audiences.

Current research that focuses on issues of class, race, and gender among school-aged girls (Gardner, Dea & McKaig 1992; Finley 1992; Luttrell 1992) supports and makes problematic the fact that many working-class girls perform multiple domestic roles for their families. Finley (1992) found that among working-class young women, aspirations of continued schooling were often squelched precisely because of the restrictions placed on them by their families in the form of domestic responsibilities at home.

In their pieces created for private audiences the girls resisted the notion that they had to give up school, school

work, and/or their friends to complete these domestic tasks
Some of the girls became spokespersons for how unfair it
was that by virtue of their gender and their economic position (since their families could not afford child care or
domestic help) they had to complete these tasks at all.
Yolanda's piece is one example:

Unfair

Unfair one day went [when] I went to church when I came
from home there were my sister's toys and when I came
my mom toll [told] me that I had to pick her toy's and I
told my mom why if I did not play with them and because
there not mine and my mom toll me to pick them up or
she was going to hit me and know [now] if she uses them
she uput them back that's all!

Yolanda began to question her purpose as a female family
member, saying to me and some of the other girls that she
just didn't think "she could do it all." Alternatively, she challenged whether performing these domestic tasks was "all
she was good for."

Follow-up discussions the girls and I had in writers'
circle to pieces like Yolanda's support the idea that the girls
were beginning to challenge roles that, in their texts for
writing workshop, they appeared to accept. For example,
in an animated conversation around getting married and
taking care of the home and the children, Lucy exclaimed,
"I'm not gonna have any babies and I'm gonna have like a
roommate." Walinda made it clear that,

"I'll have one [baby]. Cause two seems like too much
trouble. But I can have a maid, but I'll help her clean up
when I get out of work and stuff." Laurelei, too, said, "I'm
not getting married," and Nayda added, "I don't want to
have kids and I don't want to get married."

Cynthia, the girl who had written about cooking rice
and caring for her younger siblings while her mother helped
a friend, was most adamant about not accepting these multiple responsibilities, yelling out "I ain't gonna have no husband!" She continued by saying,

> Yea, I could be single because . . . you know if you're walk-
> ing with a man and he's your friend, they [husbands] like
> when you go home, then they start talking about it, they
> start fighting.

To this statement, Maribel added matter-of-factly,

> And you know I could be single because my mother said
> because when you have a husband, some husbands doesn't
> treat you like a lady. You're like garbage like when he
> says, "do this" or because he'll kill you. So for me it's better
> to be single.

These discussions around domesticity often became
very heated as the girls expressed resistant voices; voices
that teetered on the edge of anger and resentment. These
were voices that were only revealed to private audiences.

One of the other roles that most of these girls were
expected to fulfill was the role of the "caring" female sibling or daughter. For example, Chantal always felt that she
was "in the middle" of domestic quarrels between her
mother and father (who no longer lived with them), or even
between an aunt and a sibling where she always had to
negotiate squabbles. In the following writers' circle piece,
Chantal describes one such incident.

> When my sister got in trouble

> It had happed when we was over my Gandmother house.
> We was having so much fun. When we had dinner my
> aunts said to my sister to do something and she said no.
> My Aunts was going to hit her but she was running from
> her then she got on the stair, fell, then my sister said a
> bad word then she realy got it. My sister was fusing about
> my cousin was bothing her and she screaming that could
> take it. I was telling her to shut up. My Gandmother had
> said to leave her alone then I said to my Gandmother she
> is crying to much. she stop crying ate her dinner why
> everybody ate she went upstair where we was watchin
> this movie I never get a chance to watch the beging [begin-
> ning] I alway get in the middle.

Here, Chantal once again lost an opportunity to spend her free time doing what she wanted to do, uninterrupted. Instead, she sacrificed her time to mediate disputes within her family. Chantal often talked about "growing up" so that she could get out of the house and be "responsible for just herself."

Jane, too, increasingly found herself in the role of caring family member. This became especially true when her parents broke up and she felt that it was her job to get them back together. In the following journal piece, she writes about how unfair it all seems.

Unfair

The thing that unfare to me is that my Dad had to move out. I don't like it. The reason why is because? I think that this is not fair. I am traing [trying] my best to get ous [us] back togather but it is not working. This is hurting my mom bcause we dont tock [talk] to her that much. And I think my mom like some one os [else]. He allways come over and sade Hi. And I dont like it not one bit. I think that my mom is doing the rong [wrong] thing because it is hurd [hurting] all of ous. And my flamey [family] is folling apart.

Jane increasingly perceived herself as the reconciliator, trying desperately to get her parents back together, or at least get her mother away from "someone else."

Through writers' circle, oral texts, and journal entries the eleven girls in Mr. Roscoe's class were able to challenge expectations of them as primary caretakers of the home and their siblings, and that of being the nurturing female family member. Through these stories voices were heard that appeared to reflect more closely the way the girls truly felt around issues of domesticity. (These stories also allowed both Mr. Roscoe and I to develop and model critical responses to these issues. This notion of critical response to the texts in addressed more fully in chapter 9. It is important to note here, however, that the content of these stories was not ignored.)

Issues of domesticity often intertwined with other topics including other concerns of family life. These private
stories of family life revealed tensions within families that
were particularly difficult for the girls to cope with as they
began to "grow up."

Stories of Family Life

The girls reported that they felt much more comfortable writing and sharing stories about their family life in
more private contexts such as writers' circle. This was
because the girls knew that these kinds of stories were not
particularly appealing to nor valued by the boys. The girls
reported that the boys didn't share their resistance against
doing the weekly laundry, for example, and it was not
uncommon to hear the boys say things like "that's what
girls are good for."

Other concerns around family life included attempts
at resolving issues with parents about going to parties and
going out with boys. (Remember Cynthia's piece about going
to a dance with a boy in chapter 6.) These seemingly typical
adolescent issues were important for the girls to try to
understand as concrete senses of independence and freedom began to evolve.

Other family life issues, however, were much more serious and I would not have learned about them had it not
been for the private writing contexts through which the
girls knew they could speak honestly. The most frightening
written pieces around the theme of family life came from
Jane who had begun to write me a series of letters concern-
ing the breakup of her parents and the deaths of her uncle
and his girlfriend. I became very alarmed after I found in
my mailbox this first in a series of short letters to me.

Dear Brett:

I have to talk to some one But I don't know how I wont
[want] to talk to you But I don't know if you will undreside
[understand].

I responded encouraging her to tell me more and found the
following note in my mailbox the very next day:

> Thank you for the note what I was tonking [talking] about
> is I can put those suf [stuff] in my Direy and you are the
> only one to read it. My moms bother [brother] just die and
> her borther girl frind going to die that why we are moving
> and I roit [write] you.

Again, I responded and found this letter the following week:

> Dear Brett
>
> Hi It was your turn to write me Did you son come back
> [from vacation] I know my dad dind't I don't think I should
> tell you anything anymore Iam aforad [afraid] that he
> will find out. he wont if you Dont tell him. I dont know
> what Ishould do I have to talk to some one so I could let
> all this out. It is just bilding up more and more. I dont
> know why I write like this I have it I like to writ like this
> Write back.

Jane was quite reluctant to speak out loud about what
she had written in these letters and so I had to "talk" with
her through this private correspondence. As our letter writing continued I became more concerned for the great trauma
Jane was experiencing in her family life. It seems that her
uncle and her uncle's girlfriend were dying of AIDS while at
the same time her father and mother were breaking up.
These were not issues that Jane ever let become topics for
discussion outside of our correspondence. Because of the
gravity of her family life situation, however, I did inform
Mr. Roscoe while maintaining a dialogue with Jane on the
issues. Mr. Roscoe followed-up by talking to both Jane and
her mother.

Bell (1991) in a study among urban girls and a team of
multiracial researchers supports the idea that family life is
of central concern to pre-adolescent girls. It certainly was an
important topic for most of the eleven girls in Mr. Roscoe's
classroom. Sharing their concerns, tensions, unresolved con-

flicts, and grief over events in their families gave them tools to help them grow as they began to understand and cope with sensitive issues. Through private writing contexts they were validated and supported by others with similar experiences.

Evolving sexuality was another topic the girls gave great consideration to. Their understandings of their sexuality involved relationships with their families, their teachers, and particularly other boys in the classroom. As preadolescents sexuality was a crucial and timely topic that each one of the girls had an interest in.

Stories of Sexuality

Issues around sexuality were dictated to the girls in very real and frightening ways, e.g., by their families, the media, and boys. The girls often felt they were expected to be silent about being treated as sexual objects, the ridicule they incurred based on physical appearance, and as potential childbearers. The girls often felt that the burden of being female was simply unfair. Maribel was the only girl to write a piece in writing workshop that directly addressed male/female sexuality. "Puberty" was a meticulously researched "clinical" piece.

Puberty

Everybody goes thru Puberty. Puberty means were the womanhood and manhood take place. Girls go thru Puberty from 9–16 and boys thru 10–16. Girls mature first than boys grow more taller. boys arms get bigger. Girls hips widen. Girls breast start developing. Boys start to grow hair on face, under arm, and more. Girls grow hair underarm, between our legs and more. Our sex glands are ovaries and Testicles. Boys have Testicles, Girls have ovaries. Voice changes too. The boys voice gets deeper, and the girls voice will change to become lower and more richer. Girls have eggs, and boys have sperms. A woman and a Man could make a baby. It depends how

your family is that's how you grow, ~~like if your father is~~
5'7" you might grow to be 6"0 or less or more. who knoks
[knows]

Maribel, however, expressed a different voice when
writing in her journal. In the following piece about menarche and giving birth, a profound sense of inequity is
revealed.

> Girls have their periods. And I was thinking that nothing
> happens to boys and that's not fair. only girls have to pass
> the pain, and womans when their pregnant specially. I
> have a baby brother and do you know all the pain my
> mother felt. But she was ok. I was so happy to have a lit-
> tle brother. The periods of the girls are groce [gross] very
> groce. And I think it happens 1 day every month!

The fear and concerns about puberty, menarche, and
childbirth were pale, however, compared to the intense fear
most of the girls felt about getting pregnant, getting raped,
or entering into an abusive relationship. These were
extremely important issues for these girls because they felt
that they had the potential of becoming reality. And yet,
most of their questions surrounding these issues went unan-
swered since there was no nurse in the school nor family
members at home to offer guidance.

Laurelei, in the following journal entry, illustrates
clearly how critical it was that the girls had no one to talk to.

> My mother's cuison She's 15 she wen't out with a man
> but she didn't have a baby because she use condoms. and
> she still told her mother she did it. she was dom she
> shouldn't told her mother because she didn't get pregnant
> and her mother hit her and then she wen't to her room
> and try to kill herself the ambulance came her mother is
> my mothers ant by my mother's mom and I don't know no
> more!

Laurelei had decided as had most of the other girls that it was
best not to even attempt to talk to one's mother about issues

such as birth control, condom use, or unwanted pregnancy. The one piece of information that most of the girls did learn from their families was that boys were "only after one thing." Because of this, many of the girls' fathers, in particular, were reluctant to allow them to continue onto high school and/or college. During a discussion that ensued in writers' circle about these issues of birth control, condom use, pregnancy, among other things, Laurelei was quick to explain her father's position:

> My father don't want me like to, from 8th grade, go to college or something because he thinks that maybe I'm gonna come with my big stomach or something. I dunno why he thinks that, maybe a lot of girls have babies in school or something. I just tell him that no I am gonna go and he says no and I say oh yea and he says no. My mom she told me, 'ah, he's crazy.' I don't talk back or anything, I just say I'm gonna go. He said he'd kill me, then he wants to laugh. Mom just says I have to take care of myself and everything and give myself my place—I dunno. Like when I grow up and someone talks to me nice, don't be a fool and go with them, they just talk, they just want us to get pregnant. Right?

Maribel, too, had been told by her father that "bad things" happen to girls in high school and college. She joined in the discussion by saying:

> Yea, I have a question. When you go to college and you're walking by sometimes, come a boy and start bugging you, you know raping you, what do you do? I hate that, they tell you to get out of college and have fun, this 'n that, but how . . . ?

Again it was through the girls' discussions and writing that they were not only able to sort out and begin to understand the complexities of their sexuality but also to resist others' expectations of them (getting pregnant, for example). They did this by discussing issues with me and other girls, thereby at least beginning to *name* the issues as well as learn-

ing to question the validity or sense of particular expectations. (For example, we discussed and contrasted issues of
being "bugged" and being raped. Maribel, in particular, as a
result wanted to do more research on issues around rape and
with the librarian's help found a book on "date rape.")

Other voices began to emerge in discussions and texts
around sexuality; voices that experimented with language
and with ideas that the girls knew to be taboo in public
forums. An understanding of taboo topics was firmly
ingrained into the girls' heads as they constantly explained
and complained to me that even though they desperately
needed to know certain things, other females, e.g., their
mothers, classroom teachers were not "allowed" (by hus-
bands or school authorities, for example) to talk about these
things to them. These texts helped the girls to begin to not
only organize facts, for example, about sex, but also to
experiment with feelings around their own potential sexuality. One way this was done was to write and share "trick
notes" (the girls' term, not mine).

A trick note is one that is written by a ghostwriter.
Trick notes were almost always written to boys. The language in the trick notes was often quite graphic as the girls
tried out words and phrases they had heard on television,
video, or in music.

Chantal was one of the great trick note writers in the
classroom. The following piece remains unedited.

> Dear A (popular Latino boy in classroom),
>
> When I think of you it want me to do sex with you are so sexy
> I dream I didnt [did it] with you when you put your dick in
> my pussy it was so good I want more and I could stop. You
> felt so good we had 15 kid and we still do so bad that my
> pussy had turn red. Your dick went in to my mouth that I
> want you to do all the sex in the world. My sexy boy. My
> always sexy boy. We do it good. Sincerly, your sexy Emire!

Chantal's trick note mirrored what she knew and understood about her own sexuality from television, movies, and
other popular culture artifacts like rap music. As a result,

she made dangerous assumptions, for example, about connections between sex and having children and about having unprotected sex. Using various "forbidden" words gave her a sense of false control and it was only through follow-up discussions in writers' circle that these issues were elaborated upon and clarified.

Other issues of sexuality presented themselves through the words some of the boys in the classroom used toward the girls when they were upset in some way by them. The boys' perceptions of the girls were made quite clear by the use of these words, and the girls, although not physically hurt, were able to begin to articulate in writers' circle discussions their pain over such racist and sexist sexually-charged talk.

The remarks the boys used most often referred to a part of a girl's body. To add further insult to a statement as "you fat ass bitch," boys would tag a word that reflected the girl's ethnic heritage to the phrase. As Chantal explained,

> those boys when they get mad always call girls names—
> me they call a black bitch or a white nigger. I just slap
> their face.

For the Latina girls, this name calling meant that "Puerto Rican" or "Mexican" was added to the front of the word "bitch." According to Lucy being called a "Puerto Rican bitch" was not uncommon. For Laurelei who was considered overweight, the name-calling became even more fierce. It was not uncommon for me to hear her referred to by the boys as a "fat Spic." Jane, one of the few Anglas in the entire school, did not escape this sexist and racist name-calling. She reported that the boys called her, "a priceless white whore," or simply a "bitch."

Only one girl, however, responded to this sexist talk in writing. Laurelei, in a letter she wrote to Mr. Roscoe detailing events where certain boys reduced her to tears with their name-calling, eventually hitting her when she walked away, she questioned why boys had to act and speak this way. Other girls simply rather wanted to talk about like kinds of incidents in writers' circle.

The discussions around name-calling proceeded very slowly at first as both I and the girls learned that they did not understand words like "racism" and "sexism." (I had assumed they did and was surprised to learn the opposite. According to Chou's research (June 1994, personal communication) students at this age *not* knowing about racism and sexism is quite typical.) They all agreed, however, that they had experienced discrimination and abuse (whether orally or physically) based on their gender and ethnic/linguistic heritages. It was in this very important way that the girls were able to begin to name the nature of sexism and racism, a crucial first step in their *beginning*, then, to challenge and resist sexism and racism through their own voices.

Summary

The eleven girls in Mr. Roscoe's classroom sought voices of their own through writing and through those voices often resisted. Yet, these voices were not necessarily apparent within the public context of the writing workshop. It was only outside of the workshop, away from the boys and Mr. Roscoe, that the girls found the spaces to express these resistant voices.

Having opportunities to write and talk in more private contexts and for more private audiences was an extremely important avenue by which they began to name, question, resist, and even become angry over expectations and/or perceptions others held of them. These expectations and perceptions were revealed through their writing and talk around themes such as domesticity, family life, and sexuality. In these contexts, the entire process of writing was infused with a process of coming to their own voices. Writing had the potential of becoming a site for struggles over power, identity, sexuality, race, and gender. The girls began, in private spaces, to find voices of their own.

The next chapter expands on the girls' searches for their own voices amidst their exposure to and experience in an increasingly violent urban world. I will argue that it is imperative that girls' experimentation with violent voices are used as avenues to search for *solutions* to violence while their other voices (e.g., voices of activism) are cultured and nurtured as peaceful alternatives.

8

Private Writing Contexts II:
Violence and Activism

Writing is one of the ways I participate in struggle—one of the ways I help to keep vibrant and resilient that vision has kept the Family going on. Through writing I attempt to celebrate the tradition of resistance, attempt to tap [Black] potential, and try to join the chorus of voices that argues that exploitation and misery are neither inevitable nor necessary. Writing is one of the ways I participate in the transformation . . . writing is one of the ways I do my work in the world. (Bambara 1980, p. 154)

Near-Northwest Elementary School is one of the poorest schools in the city (Kozol 1991). But poverty is only one of the daily realties that each one of the eleven girls in Mr. Roscoe's classroom faced. Violence had become the girls' worst fear. And violence was a debilitating fear; a fear that many of the girls felt they simply could not escape.

Although these girls were learning to express their voices through writing in a range of ways and through a range of contexts and genres, more powerful violent voices threatened to overtake and replace them altogether. These violent voices were modeled for the girls in popular culture, including rap music and television, and also in the behaviors of the mostly male gangs in their communities.

In this chapter I will argue two interrelated dimensions of one major point. First, it is crucial to transform these violent voices, rather than letting the girls rationalize

93

or ignore them, into what I have called "productive" voices, voices that can, as Bambara argues, "do the work of the world." These productive voices become avenues in which the girls can search for alternatives and solutions to the violence. And second, it is imperative that the girls' voices of "activism" are nurtured and cultured—peaceful voices that are potentially more productive. Critical attention must be paid to both the voices of violence and the alternative voices girls developed to understand and search for options to the violence engulfing them.

Ignoring and Rationalizing Violence

As the school year progressed, the girls' writing and oral discussions focused increasingly on the issue of violence. Violence came in many forms for these girls, and some forms seemed less insidious than others. The reality was, however, that the girls' exposure to and experience of violence was beginning to silence them even further. Ignoring the violence was just one way in which they became increasingly silent.

One way in which violence was modeled for the girls was through music, particularly rap music. Rap music, like other forms of popular culture available to pre-adolescents (e.g., television, video), functions as an additional "meaning system or discourse . . . where individual identities are formed" (Ang 1992, p. 84). Rap music is essentially a musical genre that evolved out of young urban males' need to separate from "mainstream" culture. It is also a genre whose lyrics are often sexist, racist, and violent (Prothrow-Stith 1991). Pre-adolescents frequently make powerful connections between the lyrics of a rap song, for example, and their own lives. It was the music of choice among Mr. Roscoe's students, including the girls.

Walinda was a heavy consumer of rap and hip hop music. It was not uncommon for her to share her music with me as she asked my opinion about certain dance moves, or whether I knew the difference between rap and hip hop (I

didn't then but I do now). I didn't often pay much attention
to the lyrics of a particular song until one day when Walinda
brought in an actual tape and asked permission to play it on
my tape recorder. Some of the titles and lyrics read, "Shoot
the Bitch," "Up a girl's ass," and "Pop that pussy." The following discussion took place with Walinda and Jane, who
had joined in the dancing and singing:

> BRETT: Do you think it's cool for men to talk about women
> like that?
>
> JANE: Yeah.
>
> WALINDA: I dunno Brett, I never really thought about it.
>
> BRETT: Well we're gonna talk about it . . . (I am inter-
> rupted by a boy who begins to speak)
>
> BOY: Yea, I can write like that. (The boys knew too that I
> was interested in writing.)

When we were able to continue our discussion about
the dangerously violent and sexist lyrics, Walinda and Jane
made it clear that listening to rap music was something
"everyone" did; it was accepted. No one had ever attempted
to explain why such language may be harmful and these
two girls did not really see a problem with it. The violent,
sexist language was reinforced by the boys in their classroom through their writing and conversations. The girls
seemed to ignore this kind of language.

This became even more clear when, during an Author's
Chair, two boys (one of whom had interrupted my discussion
with Walinda and Jane) shared the following piece called,
"Killer Boys."

Killer Boys

It was some boys that they thought they were bad, they
were 21 years old. So evey time some one would look at
them and they would kill them. So one time a cop tryed
to get one of the killer boys. So the cop shot him, he shot
him in the leg so two of the killer boys came and killed
the cop, two of the killer boys came and took the one

that got shot to the hospital. So one time a old ladie looked at them and they killed the old ladie . . . So [we] took out a gun so we left to our car and got some guns then we waited in it till they came, a old ladie came out of the alley and they raipt her and killed her, so I went over and they throw the old ladie in a garbage can . . . then we went to our limo and we went to pack up the babes and we went to are castle and we went to sleep with them in the badroom, the names of the girl's were . . .

The boys shared their opinions on this piece with each other, laughing and joking throughout the Author's Chair discussion. Laurelei was the only girl to finally speak. Excerpts of the discussion follow:

AUTHOR 1: (in response to question by another boy) Did we go to bed with the girls?

BOY IN AUDIENCE: Yea, you could do that to a 6 year old girl?

AUTHOR 1: No, the girls are 11 and 12 years old.

AUTHOR 2: They're bad [killer boys] this is about the killer boys and they get the girls cause they're bad.

MR. ROSCOE: I don't get the ending.

BOY IN AUDIENCE: Yea, good guys killed bad guys and got the girls.

LAURELEI: It's maybe 'cause they're [the girls] only going with them 'cause they're prostitutes. (Laughter.)

In this example, Laurelei was the only girl to speak. All of the rest of the girls (including myself) ignored this form of violence by remaining silent. And yet Laurelei spoke up, rationalizing the violent sexism by stating that only prostitutes would go with the "killer boys." In other words, there must be something wrong with the *girls*, not the boys. (See chapter 9 for a fuller discussion on "response" in Mr. Roscoe's classroom).

Rationalizing violence was a common tactic among the
eleven girls in Mr. Roscoe's classroom. This rationalization
was most apparent through the writing they did for public
use. For example, as previously discussed in chapter 5, in
apology notes, the girls attempted to explain away the disruptive behavior of the boys. In doing this, they either tried
to take some of the "blame" for the violence, or tried to persuade others that this violence was so routine that it simply
could no longer be helped.

For example, Teresa, like many of the other girls,
attempted to rationalize the violent behavior of the boys by
saying that when it got hot, they fought.

> Dear Mrs. Brett,
>
> I am very sorry for our class that were fighting and doing
> everything they want. I'am very sorry that, that happen in
> this class think that, that happen because is hot because a
> very [every] year that is hot there's a fight. Sincerely, Teresa

To Teresa, the violence had simply become an "it," an
"it" so routine that it was accepted as part of their daily
lives. It was not something that they thought I should
accept, however, and they wrote notes to me saying I didn't
deserve such treatment. Yolanda wrote:

> Dear Mrs. Brett
>
> I'm really sorry for the 4 fights on your last day. I apol-
> lagice. I'm really sorry. I am shure [sure] that they are
> going to appolacis [apologize] because you don't decirve
> [deserve] that, because you are a very good person. Sin,
> [sincerely] Yolanda

In public, then, the girls tried to either ignore, dismiss,
or rationalize the violence around them as part of their daily
lives; routines that simply could not be questioned nor alle-
viated. For private audiences, however, the girls began to
express concern over violence. One way they accomplished
this was to experiment with violent voices of their own.

Transforming Violent Voices into Productive Voices

Fight Stories

The violence that urban adolescents are exposed to in their daily lives is supported by the discovery that among the girls Shuman (1986) worked with, "fight stories" always elicited the "longest written works produced" (p. 148). Fight stories are retellings of actual events and are used by urban adolescents as ways to not only present accounts, but also to dispute or settle the accounts of certain violent events. In this way, the storyteller is able to practice, experiment, and find solutions, through language, to violence.

One way the girls in Mr. Roscoe's classroom used fight stories was as avenues in which they could express concern over the violence around them. They did this by experimenting with violent voices of their own and then talking directly about the violence, i.e., how it started, how it stopped, how it might have been stopped in group discussions. Fight stories were always presented in private contexts in either written or oral texts. Often the oral retelling of an incident led to a later written account.

Walinda was a prolific producer of fight stories. Whether or not she was involved in the fracas she was often the first girl to begin an oral account of who, what, why, when, and how. On this particular day, during a writers' circle meeting in the hallway, she begins our meeting with a retelling of her sister's involvement in a fight that included herself and her classmate, Nayda:

> I guess some girls were banging on Nayda's door yesterday after school, so my sister came and said ain't gonna be no 6 on my sister—you get two, we get two. See Lorraine [girl in another class] was coming up to Nayda's face and when her brother came up she even tried to act bad. So Nayda pushed her back after Lorraine pushed her.

At this point, Lucy jumps in to add to the story, and the story continues among the entire group of girls,

LUCY: Yea and Lorraine drops her notebook and says to
me . . . so then I said, 'I don't have to take this' and walk
away. Cause look it, it was like this. They called me. So
then Walinda was by my house and then we went to
school and then . . .

NAYDA: Is that the time they start to fight?

WALINDA: Yea, and everyone was gathered. And this is
how small the circle was with me and my sister (gestures
to our writers' circle.)

BRETT: Just like this?

WALINDA: Yea, and everyone was starting to gather.

LUCY: Dig!

WALINDA: Everyone was sqooshed and everythin . . .

CHANTAL: Lucy, you got a mouth . . .

BRETT: So, does she [Lorraine] get out-of-school suspen-
sion?

As the discussion continued, Chantal, myself, and some of
the other girls wanted explanations as to why the fight
started and solutions as to how it could have been avoided
altogether. "Walking away" was mentioned most as a viable
alternative. The oral accounts of the fight were eventually
turned into a short journal entry by Lucy as a way, perhaps, to help her more clearly sort out the events,

> The fight was on Jan 20, 1993 they start to fight until
> Lorraine's brother came to Brake it up. Lorraine and Nayda
> were fighting. Nayda was fighting with one hand because
> she had her books in her in her had [in her other hand].

Other fight stories resulted from disagreements among
the eleven girls themselves. (This was rare, though, as the
girls presented a strong, solid community in which there
was little in-fighting.) In these fight stories too, the girls
experimented both with the possibilities of violence and
solutions to violence.

A few days after the incident with Lorraine and
Walinda's sister, Walinda and Lucy began to argue over a

pen, eventually striking each other in the classroom. When Mr. Roscoe asked me to take them into the hallway to discuss the incident, a "fight story" retelling occurred. The girls' retelling was most notable in that it included an attempt at *solutions* and *alternatives* to the violence. Excerpts of these attempts follow:

> WALINDA: I get mad too easy.
>
> BRETT: You get what?
>
> WALINDA: I get mad fast.
>
> BRETT: Yea, I get mad fast and you know what I have to do? *Walk away*. What can you try to do?
>
> WALINDA: Not get mad.
>
> BRETT: But how?
>
> WALINDA: Walk away.
>
> LUCY: Let her use the pen. (pause) I forgot what happened! (laughs).

The actual retelling allowed the girls to critically look at what happened and why. Lucy, in the end, hadn't even remembered the exact incidents leading up to the violence. This helped her understand that the whole event may have been quite inconsequential, and thus, avoidable.

Fight stories also allowed some of the girls to examine *feelings* around particular violent incidents. For example, Laurelei felt that all those around her were talking and gossiping about her. She felt quite powerless to do anything about the gossip, except through her writing. (Remember the personal note to Mr. Roscoe about the boys' name-calling.) In her writers' circle journal, she began to create her own scenarios, approximating fight stories of her own. In the following journal piece, she stands up to her attackers saying,

> Write [right] know [now] after we come from lunch Walinda and Lucy I swear with all your respect I am gonna kik their ass! and any if they call my mother she won' care she told me that if they bother me to kik their

ass. and you [know] that Yolanda is my frind write [right?]
Well when she in front of Lucy and Lucy is talking about
me, she does too.

Laurelei's experimentation with a violent voice through a
fight story helped her to examine her feelings of vulnerabil-
ity. This appeared to help her to feel stronger and in control.

Shuman (1986) claims that "fight stories often were
more essential than the physical contact itself" (p. 95).
This appeared to be true among the eleven girls in Mr.
Roscoe's class as they used the opportunities "fight stories" presented to describe and discuss the violence
around them, to examine their feelings, and to search for
solutions to such violence. These productive voices helped
them to perhaps cope as the violence around them was
very real.

The reality of violence the girls experienced became
even more clear to me through their oral stories of gangs
and violence in their neighborhoods. All of the girls in Mr.
Roscoe's classroom claimed to know at least one gang member and it was not uncommon for them to point out members of certain gangs to me. There was a real fear of these
boys and increasingly in writers' circle discussions, the issue
was raised.

Gang Violence

One afternoon near the end of the school year, Maribel,
Alejandra, and I sat in the hallway talking about their
future as writers in sixth grade and beyond into junior high
and high school. This is the way the discussion evolved as
Alejandra interrupted saying,

Yea, I used to have a best friend. I had one but she died,
her name was Antoinette. They shot her in the heart. She
was 10. She was in the park and they shot her last year
when it was Puerto Rican day. They shot her.

Alejandra continued by telling me her mother did not want
her, therefore, to go to high school at all, adding,

My mom doesn't want to put me in high school 'cause now the other last time, they almost shot my brother. There was a fight with the gangsters and they were doing shots and my brother they shot him and he was in the hospital and they took the bullet out . . . My mother says [by the time I get to high school] I'm not going be here, 'cause we're going to Puerto Rico.

At this point in the discussion, as Maribel and I sat transfixed by these stories, Maribel added a loud, "Me too."

Our talk continued well into the afternoon as the girls tried to make sense of living in such a violent world. They shared our concerns over our futures and the future of our families and tried to come up with additional options. "Walking away" (i.e., leaving the city) was again considered to be the number one solution. Writing letters to television executives and boycotting violent television shows were also contemplated. The girls' deeply concerned voices echoed throughout the oral texts they created around such a violent life.

Thus, experimentation with violent voices modeled after popular culture and the gang members in their communities served a crucial purpose in the girls' expression of voice. Primarily, such experimentation allowed the girls to learn to question issues of violence and to transform these issues into solutions. Rather than allowing others' violent voices to overrun them, they found ways to channel them into more productive voices.

Voices of Activism: Peaceful Voices

Other more peaceful voices began to emerge later in the school year as well. As the girls matured and began to understand, perhaps, their communities more clearly, and the opportunities writing gave them to talk about their communities, peaceful, "activist" voices could be heard. These peaceful voices truly represented voices of their own.

Lensmire (1994) talks of the need for students to develop and express two very distinct kinds of voices through their writing: an artistic voice and a political voice. An artistic voice, he tells us, aims to name and express oneself. A political voice aims to name the world.

Female professional writers (Bambara 1980; Cisneros cited in Tabor 1993; Lourde 1984; Morrison cited in Micucci 1992; and Wolf 1929) have always spoken of a woman's need, in particular, to culture a voice that is not only productive and peaceful, but one that speaks out against daily injustices both against oneself and the world. Toward the end of the school year, some of the girls in Mr. Roscoe's classroom, both through public and private writing contexts, began to name and identify certain injustices through their writing, often becoming strong advocates for particular issues and ideas they believed in.

Lucy, for example, became through her writing, an animal rights activist. She began to write a series of pieces on cheetahs and dolphins, explaining her cause in writers' circle this way,

> I like to write about animals and freedom and stuff like that. Like those poor butterflies [kept in a box in the classroom]. You know, animal rights and stuff. Yea, because those poor dolphins, I mean they make tuna out of them!

She subsequently wrote a well-researched piece on the plight of the cheetahs for Author's Chair,

> Cheetahs are a very large cat with spots that is something like a leopard and is found in Southern Asia and Africa. Cheetahs run very fast and are fastest animal in the world. Also they are called hunting leopards. Either of two cat [is] native from India to Africa, south of the Sahrara. The common cheetahs stand about 3 feet tall at the shoulder and measure 6 feet long from it's nose. But the cheetahs are in danger from man and this is terrible. Something should be done.

Because Lucy was so concerned about these animals, she began to experiment with other genres to express her deep interest. She reports that the following poem highlights her feelings of attachment to these creatures.

Cheetahs
Big, fast,
Kill, fight, jump
Cheetahs are so cool
Nice.

Other kinds of activist writing, too, became apparent in both the girls' public and private spheres. Cynthia, for example, befriended a homeless woman, bringing her food on a daily basis. This effort on Cynthia's part was extremely moving since Cynthia's family itself was very poor. Cynthia had developed a voice of passion and decency as the following piece clearly shows.

> The day I found 200 hundres dollars in the street and I saw a little poor woman and she could not talk and my mom told me to give the money to the poor woman so I did. She give me a cros of Jesus and she was nice. I was the only one who gave her alot of money and I star [started] to bringing food to her she live in an old house the one day it got brend [burned] and so we take her to os [our] house and her room was in the atic and every time she go to my house to eat and take a bath and change.

Many of the girls spoke about similar incidents of trying to help elderly, poor people in their community, abandoned babies, relatives, and even homeless animals. Although their voices are not necessarily sophisticated, the girls, both through their oral and written texts, began to express these voices of compassion and understanding, aimed at beginning to name and deal with in very concrete ways, the injustices of the world.

Summary

In Mr. Roscoe's classroom private writing contexts gave the eleven girls opportunities in which they could both experiment with violent voices and move toward more peaceful and productive voices as the school year unfolded.

These voices began to mirror the activist voices of famous female authors, for example, as the girls began to name and offer solutions to, the violence and injustices they increasingly were exposed to in their daily lives.

There are two major foci in the next chapter. First, I show how important it is for teachers of writing to not only create the opportunities necessary for expressing girls' varied and multiple voices, but also to provide critical responses to the actual texts that girls, in particular, produce. (I have called these texts "cultural texts," texts that I believe should form the literature of the classroom).

First, however, I believe it crucial to study (for comparison, contrast, and discussion) boys' voices and responses so that we can better study girls' voices and responses. Teachers may allow for experimentation with a range of voices through a range of genres and contexts while nurturing and culturing *all* the voices that are heard. In this way, girls' voices can become powerful voices on the edge of adolescence, as they are validated, challenged, expressed, shared, and respected.

9

Becoming Critical:
The Importance of Modeling Responses
to Cultural Texts

. . . writing activities and texts are part of the social life of
the classroom: they respond to the workshop context, but
also partially constitute that context and shape future
activities and texts. Teacher response to children's texts
also participates in this social life . . . Our response to
children's texts, then, must be critically pragmatic and
must consider the intellectual, moral/political, and aes-
thetic fruits of children's work and teacher response—and
not only for the children we happen to be talking to face-
to-face. (Lensmire 1993, p. 266)

The purpose of this chapter is many-layered. The major
focus is to highlight the manner in which the boys' voices
and responses affected the girls' voices and responses in profound, and often, frightening ways. To do this, I have provided a closer glimpse of the boys' voices as seen through
the lens of "reader response," exploring such central questions as: How do we (as educators) validate (and should we
validate) the mostly-male responses in the classroom? In
other words, how do we contribute to the girls' silences even
further if we only accept and critically examine boys'
responses? And finally, then, how do we create new ways to
respond in a "critically pragmatic" way so that girls are not
afraid to speak and so that their voices, too, are validated?
Specifically, here, I will expand on what I mean by "cultural texts" and "critical response" framing the first within

a Bakhtinian perspective and the second within the current theoretical contexts in which "response" is viewed. Next, by providing examples of texts and responses to those texts, I hope to not only show how the students, but also how Mr. Roscoe and I, responded to these sample student texts. Our responses help to elucidate how much further we needed to go in learning to question and challenge, and even formulate, the "critically pragmatic" responses Lensmire (1993) writes about, particularly as we cultivated the girls' voices through response.

Critical Response to Cultural Texts

What are Cultural Texts?

According to Bakhtin (1981, 1986) the act of composing is always an act of "dialogism." That is, when a writer uses words, she "necessarily engages or responds to past and present discourses," as each word "smells of the context . . . in which it has lived its intense social life" (Ewald 1993, p. 332). A cultural text is a text which "smells" of a particular context or contexts. Among urban writers, it is a text, perhaps, that releases scents of gender, race, and class; a text that reflects their particular aspirations, struggles, and realities.

An emphasis, therefore, needs to be placed on not only *how* the text is socially and culturally constructed from such notions as gender, race, and class, but on *what* the text actually says, revealing issues of gender, race, and class that are particularly central to urban, poor students. These issues, then, form the literature of the classroom and both students and teacher can use such texts as points of critique for further discussion and examination. Cultural texts, therefore, can provide models on which others (e.g., teachers and students) can begin to name and therefore potentially change their social conditions.

And yet, cultural texts are much more than simply the texts students themselves produce. They are *what* the students bring to texts that they read; how they interpret texts, how they interact with the texts, how they react to texts, and how they make connections to the texts they read in school. Just like "good literature focuses on the lived experiences of its characters, student-generated [cultural] texts focus on the lived experiences of the students themselves" (Barone, Eeds, & Mason 1995, p. 30). The study of how students "do" all of this with text may be called "reader response."

What is Response?

Traditional Response

Reader response to literature has been examined extensively among middle-class suburban students, particularly at the secondary level (Beach & Wendler 1987; Beach & Hynds 1991; Blake 1989; Langer 1994). These explorations of students' response have focused primarily on response to "mainstream" literature. Recently, too, there have been accounts of *how* students respond to multicultural literature, with an emphasis on exploring the particular cultural stance or subject position a student takes with regard to the text (Altieri 1994; Barton 1994; Beach 1994, Enciso 1994). Oral response to literature also has been explored more carefully as "talk" in the elementary classroom has taken a more central position among the language arts (Blake 1992; Weiss, K.J., Strickland, D.S., Walmsley, S.A., & Bronk, G. 1995).

Traditional response is reflected most clearly in students' stances or subject positions toward texts. Beach (1994 a,b) describes "stances" alternately as "ideological orientations or perspectives associated with gender, class, or race, i.e., the stance of white male privilege" (p. 1) *and* "reflections of cultural models/discourses . . . acquired from social practices in specific social contexts" (p. 1). Stances reflect society. All students, then, adopt multiple, often competing stances, some of which, resist the teacher's articulated stances or stances of students perceived to be "good" students, and others that simply reflect what students are taught to believe are "good" responses.

In the classroom, students' stances are formed, in large part, based on society's assumptions. So, for example, urban students may offer responses based on judgments of the larger society of who *they* are (e.g., criminals, prostitutes, much like Laurelei's response above) and what they're capable of being (e.g., dropouts, gangsters, etc.). Urban students, simply put, often do not have the repertoire of "positive" stances and/or ideological discourses from which to write and respond as, "[urban] students have internalized self-contempt from years of official neglect . . ." (Bigelow 1990, p. 439). Their responses, often then, mirror this self-contempt and neglect.

According to Enciso (1994), however, because the cultural models on which students base their stances (and also she argues, their identities) are not necessarily well-defined (and are constantly shifting), modeling critical responses may be crucial in helping students to reshape and redefine not only their cultural stances, but their own identities. In doing this, then, students can challenge, through response, the judgments and assumptions made about them by the mainstream culture.

Critical Response

There has been relatively little research that explores the need for teachers to respond critically to students' lived experiences particularly in the form of students' oral and written texts (Lensmire 1993). Furthermore, the literature is virtually silent on reports that look at the *teacher's modeling of response* to literature (Enciso 1994) particularly among urban students responding to their own cultural texts. Yet, it is here, i.e., among urban girls I would argue, that it becomes most crucial to examine the ways in which "traditional" student responses are grounded in society's assumptions, inequities, and limits so that these inequities can be understood, and perhaps, transformed.

Lensmire (1993), in his piece on "response as socio-analysis," supports the importance of a critical response. Here, he argues that two different (i.e., non-traditional) conceptions of response need be considered; one where the teacher "follows" the child writer as the child initiates the writing and the teacher then follows her or his lead; and another where response becomes cathartic, and a way to challenge oppression. Lensmire (1993) elaborates:

> response as socioanalysis assumed that traces of racial, class, and gender oppression would at times, find their way into the stories children told. Children's texts were conceived of as artifacts of an oppressive U.S. society (similar to how, in psychoanalysis, patients' stories are viewed as artifacts of Oedipal conflicts) (p. 271).

Modeling a Critical Response

Teachers are instrumental in helping students to not only shape their cultural texts, but also to learn how to respond critically to these texts. Lensmire (1993) describes this process specifically as one where teacher and students need to, "critically examine the 'traditionally given,' and problematize claims embedded in the cultural material [we worked with as we wrote our stories]" (p. 275). Teachers need to establish a sense of community where they can not only help shape these responses, but also to become self-critical in what Bigelow (1990) has called their own, "complicity in oppression" (p. 445). Of course, this then means that the teacher needs not only to take on particular stances, but also to rigorously self-examine the stances she or he adopts.

Teachers, then, play a central role in developing and modeling a critical response for several reasons. First, modeling response may encourage students' "desire to understand and feel empathy for different people, times, and dilemmas" (Enciso 1994, p. 524). Second, a modeling of response may help students to learn to use one's own cultural resources to make connections not only with the text but with oneself. Third, response can help students to learn to "raise challenges to stereotyped interpretations of characters" (Enciso 1994, p. 527) as they move away from strict interpretations and explanations based on "mainstream culture." And finally, and perhaps most importantly, through critical response to one's own cultural texts I would argue, girls, in particular, can learn to challenge racist and sexist assumptions that pervade *their* own cultural stances and ideological positions about themselves.

"Killer Boys" and Other Stories

Responses such as those that we heard from Laurelei, Robert and Winfield in reaction to the cultural text "Killer Boys" in chapter 8 are indeed examples of the type of response that is especially crucial to reexamine in the classroom. Left on their own, these oral responses would have continued to perpetuate many potentially dangerous assumptions and stereotypes of urban boys and girls. They would have also contributed to the girls' silencing even further.

In Mr. Roscoe's classroom, responses such as those heard around cultural texts, such as the "Killer Boys," evolved both from Mr. Roscoe's modeling of types of responses over a several month period and students' greater willingness to respond more readily to their own cultural texts. In order to explore how these responses began to take shape, let me first present earlier (i.e., earlier in the school year to trade books, for example) texts and responses within the larger context of "reading workshop." I will then finish with "Killer Boys," and discuss two major, interconnected points. First, working towards a critical response to students' cultural texts in the classroom is crucial in promoting dialogue and change, however, second, much more is needed in the way of promoting and encouraging critical response by *all* students if *girls, in particular,* are going to achieve a true sense of entitlement, empowerment, and voice.

This is Boring

However bold Mr. Roscoe's students' responses may seem, they were not particularly atypical, especially late in the school year. Earlier on in the school year, however, student responses often seemed stilted and unnatural, as if the students had no clue how to nor what to respond about. Indeed like the students Kucer (1995) studied, Mr. Roscoe's students often appeared "puzzled . . . reluctant . . . limited, and unable to discuss" (p. 25) until later in the school year when "student-published texts became available . . . responses [then] became more varied and specific . . ." (p. 26).

Mr. Roscoe introduced concepts around the "reading workshop" early in the school year and, over time, reading workshop quickly took up most of the afternoon, nudging its way from a time slot in the late morning to early afternoon, and finally stretching quite often into the rest of the day. It was here, in reading workshop, that Mr. Roscoe said that he most wanted students "to make connections between what they do in the morning (i.e., write) and what they should be doing now."

The reading workshop routine always began and ended the same way: at 11:30 a.m. or so, the students were asked to take out their "reading records" and log in what they were reading, subsequently responding in writing in their "response journals;" by noon both Mr. Roscoe and I gathered small groups together to form "literature circles" to talk about each student's respective books, so that by 12:50 p.m. or so, Mr. Roscoe had usually begun a teacher read-aloud, finishing to make way for math by 1:10. Both these "large" classroom contexts provided ample opportunity for response.

In Mr. Roscoe's classroom, early responses to trade books were indeed often stilted. Nayda, for example, diligently made many such entries in her reading response journal, often simply reducing an entry to "It's boring." Here is an excerpt from her journal about a book on Congress that she was reading in the late Fall of the school year:

Dear Mr. Roscoe,

I think that the Congress is very very boring. Because when you read it, it sounds like it don't make scence [sense] so I think you shouldn't read it any more because it's very boring. Sincerely, Nayda

Mr. Roscoe found that Nayda was not the only student who often responded that she either "didn't like the book" or found it "boring." So, as a result, Mr. Roscoe, in a large group format, suggested to the class they try to respond "in a personal way, in a way that told him how they felt." This type of modeling of what the response literature calls an "affective response" (Beach & Hynds 1991) may lead students away from a pat response of "It's boring" as they bring in their own experiences to their understanding of the text. After giving several examples, Mr. Roscoe urged the students to attempt this "new" kind of response.

Nayda was successful in internalizing what Mr. Roscoe had said about responding on a personal level. Here is her reading response journal entry one month later to the book, *The World War II at Monte Cassino* (Sanford 1991).

> Dear Mr. Roscoe:
>
> When Larry was in the army he had to eat army food and he said it tasted alful and he didn't like it. When my dad wasin the army he had to eat army [food] too And he didn't like it either. What I like about this book is that it reminds me ofmy dad that's the only thing I like about this book. Well I think I'm done talking about this book.

Clearly connecting the main character's experiences in the army to those of her father, (Remember Nayda wrote prolifically about her father and his leaving the family in chapter 4). Nayda was able to take what she otherwise considered "boring stuff" and turn parts of the book into something she could admittedly like, e.g., "the only thing I like about this book . . ."

Family Values

Teacher read-aloud was another important context for response. As part of his "bridge" across reading and writing curricula, Mr. Roscoe set aside at least twenty minutes a day to read aloud to his students. On this particular day, midway through the school year, Mr. Roscoe was finishing

Indian in the Cupboard (Reid 1980). Mr. Roscoe, originally trained in the theater, was a masterful reader, engaging the students and myself into trance-like states-of-mind. On this day, as he finished reading, he admonished his students not to perform a particular ritual that the characters in the book had performed. In this excerpt of the oral responses of the large group, Mr. Roscoe began:

> MR. R.: Anybody want to say anything? Don't go trying this blood brother stuff [cutting each other's finger and sharing the blood], book wasn't written in this day and age with AIDS!
>
> MR. R.: What did you think of the ending?
>
> WILLIE: Good ending, that way they can make another one.
>
> MR. R.: A sequel . . . Is this a part you didn't understand?
>
> MR. R.: What about the lessons of life here?
>
> WILLIE: About how the family acts . . . ?
>
> MR. R.: Family values . . .
>
> DARIUS: Well, they shouldn't put [that] in there.
>
> MR. R.: Why?
>
> MR. R.: I'll tell you the part I didn't like. She [author] wrote in Bright Stars [lead female character] like as a servant to men and I didn't like that. Remember though the story was written in a time when women were practically bred to be servants . . .
>
> WILLIE: Yea, she never said a word, like the silent slave.

Notice the attention Mr. Roscoe places first on "family values," a theme he quickly moves away from, in favor of what he considered to be a theme warranting a more critical response: the stereotypic nature of the lead female character. (This is what "good" response is supposed to do: move in natural directions toward issues and themes that seem to warrant a more critical eye). The entire dialogue served to work, again, as a model as to how, or in what direction one could take in talking about, or responding to a book.

At first glance, the entire episode, too, looked as though it could serve to model as to not only *how,* but also as to *what* kind of themes and issues are okay to talk about or respond to. We thought that as students may not yet have the words to describe stereotypes or sexism, for example, they might certainly begin to have the words to question issues around gender, race, and class if these topics were presented to them as valid and important ones that should and can be discussed. On closer analysis, however, we began to see that what we were doing (by validating these responses) was to clearly say to the girls that boys' concerns such as a "bloodbrother ritual" were far more important than any issues they may have. Talking about the female character as a "slave" was only an afterthought, and even then a seemingly "male" interpretation was ascribed to it.

Under Age?

A typical literature circle with its small size (four students and one adult, for example) is another good place where students can learn and feel comfortable with, response. As a result, literature circles are a good context in which to model a critical response.

Shortly after winter break during February of the school year, Mr. Roscoe asked me to conduct a literature circle with four students: Darius, an African-American boy who was reading a biography on Ben Franklin; Hector, African-American, and boastful that he "never does his homework," who was reading a biography on Martin Luther King, Jr.; Peter, a Latino who was re-reading a book on Babe Ruth, and Walinda; the only girl in the group, who was reading a piece about the United States Constitution. Before I had had even a chance to go around the group to see who was reading what, Darius had begun to speak, telling Peter of little known important facts about Babe Ruth to which *he* was privy. (Excerpts from audiotaped transcriptions follow:)

> DARIUS: His father was a big sturdy man, and all the policemen came in, he was sent to reform school.

BRETT: So he went to reform school just for getting in a fight?

DARIUS: Yea, the restaurant got messed up and he was acting all bad and everything and there was this lady, I think she lived next door she came up. She said 'why don't you just put him in the school? Cause they have better chances and stuff.'

BRETT: Why would you have a better chance in a reform school?

HECTOR: Cause it's like they treat you better.

BRETT: Doing what?

DARIUS: Cause he was having a bad time when he was staying here. When he got there, he met this man . . .

PETER: [Retakes conversation and begins to read facts from his book]

BRETT: How long was he in reform school?

PETER: From 1902 to 1914.

BRETT: 12 years?

DARIUS: That's where he learned to play baseball!

PETER: [Continues to read, comes across word "underprivileged"]

BRETT: Anybody know what "underprivileged" means?

HECTOR: Under age?

PETER: Something about not being mature.

DARIUS: Like if you get privileges, you get extra things that you like.

BRETT: Right! So, if you're underprivileged?

DARIUS: You don't get all the things that you like.

Indeed, in this literature circle issues around race, class, and gender did surface; issues that should and could be responded to. Although here the responses did not evolve beyond than defining terms, the discussion itself did set the stage for students to begin to grapple with terms like "underprivileged." This quickly became evident later within the same literature circle as Hector, while reading aloud to the group from his book on Martin Luther King, came across the word, "Negro." Rather than skipping this word, however, it was addressed. This is how:

> HECTOR: [Reading] . . . famous Negro?
>
> BRETT: What does that mean, 'Negro?'
>
> HECTOR: Black person.
>
> BRETT: Why do they use that in the book?
>
> HECTOR: I dunno.
>
> HECTOR: Maybe 'cause they wrote the book when he was born.
>
> BRETT: Ok, let's find out when the book was written . . .
>
> DARIUS: 1968, No wait that's 'copyright," so it'd be before that . . .
>
> WALINDA: Like Rosa Parks . . . [using word 'Negro']
>
> BRETT: Do you think that's right?
>
> HECTOR/DARIUS: Nope.
>
> DARIUS: I would stick them in their face. [for using word 'Negro.']

Again, although the student responses seemed very narrowly constrained around defining and using a term like "Negro," words such as "underprivileged" and "Negro" were not ignored. Notice, however, Walinda's relative silence.

Women's Days

Most of the girls' responses still were made in private, small group contexts; the girls neither appropriated the boys' voices or responses for large groups, nor did they share their own in such contexts. They simply knew that their responses and voices were not valid in or outside of the classroom, a phenomenon clearly highlighted in the above excerpts of literature circle where Walinda (usually quite vocal and animated) was virtually silent.

In an attempt to alleviate this "problem," i.e., the girls' not sharing and responding to texts, Mr. Roscoe and I devised something called "women's days." In retrospect, we understood it to be a superficial attempt at giving girls their own days in which to speak, as it quickly became apparent that it was simply a "bandaid" that we applied to ease their "victimization." The girls looked upon it as a punishment.

Women's days were alternating days of the week (Tuesdays and Thursdays, for example) where during Author's Chair or response time to a Read Aloud, only the girls could respond. This gave the girls opportunities, we thought, to not only be prepared to respond, but to know that they would be given the space and time to do so. Further, Mr. Roscoe made it clear to the girls that he would not allow the boys to interrupt, to make fun of, nor to silence them. This is how the idea for "women's days" came about during a large group discussion and response around a book Mr. Roscoe had been reading aloud. (Notice his frustration in trying to model just how these women's days might be conducted.)

> MR. ROSCOE: How would you predict the ending? (Two boys respond.)
>
> MR. ROSCOE: What happened women? I'm tired, the women don't make enough comments in this class—(calls on a girl who shrugs her shoulder and does not respond.)
>
> MR. ROSCOE: C'mon, let's hear some women!
>
> BOY: They ain't women!
>
> MR. ROSCOE: Who said that?
>
> LAURELEI: Well, I would predict that . . .
>
> MR. ROSCOE: That's a good prediction. (Boys from audience jump in and continue to dominate responses.)
>
> MR. ROSCOE: C'mon women, let's have some comments! I know, maybe we should have men's response day and women's! (Cheers). Starting next week, Tuesdays and Thursdays will be women's day.

Although well-intended, the idea of having "women's days" was too difficult for most of the girls to deal with, and most of

them continued to be non-responsive in the large group setting. It had become clear to me, however, that the girls
weren't responding because they had nothing to say; they
weren't responding because they felt that no matter what
Mr. Roscoe did, the boys wouldn't value their responses. As a
result, the majority of the girls did not respond aloud to anything, regardless of "women's day." (Laurelei seemed to be
the only exception throughout the countless Author's Chairs,
read alouds, and literature circles I observed and participated
in. See again the responses around "Killer Boys" in chapter 8).

The Killer Boys: Future Directions for Response

However far we thought the students had come in
learning to respond critically to books and stories and to
their own generated cultural texts, oral responses like those
heard around the text, "Killer Boys," reminded both Mr.
Roscoe and myself just how far we all needed to go. That is,
as the boys became more courageous; trying out stories, perhaps, designed to "tell it like it is;" to shock, the responses,
particularly from the girls, became less courageous.

There were two major reasons for this reaction. First,
although we had begun to add to the students' repertoire of
response by helping them to become critical on certain levels
and around certain issues, not enough modeling of a variety of
critical responses had yet taken place. Mr. Roscoe and I had
barely begun to scratch the surface in responding to issues
around race and gender, for example, as we ourselves were
just learning to unravel and explore assumptions about who
poor, urban students were. We had not yet begun, then, to present alternative reactions to all of these "traditional" assumptions. And, more crucially, we had not yet moved far enough in
problematizing and examining *our own* assumptions; a step
we needed to take before and while students were examining
and challenging such traditional assumptions. This, in turn, led
us to validate the boys' voices in lieu of the girls'.

Second, we had not yet created enough "safe" spaces
where girls, in particular, could try out these new assump-

tions in the form of response. We had clearly guided both
girls and boys to learn to compose their own texts, and to
respond in a variety of ways to both trade books and to their
own cultural texts. We were heartened by the fact that like
the reports in the research we had read (see especially,
Kucer 1995), the students' cultural texts promoted the most
varied and numerous responses. And we were pleased that
at least in one area the girls' responses began to noticeably
take on a critical edge was around the issues of domesticity,
marriage, and childbearing. (See chapter 7 for an earlier
discussion of these themes). As the school year progressed,
and the girls felt increasingly comfortable with challenging
such traditional assumptions, their responses (albeit in
small, private group contexts) to expectations and perceptions of them became more detailed, specific, and powerful.
(For example, see Cynthia and Maribel's stories around why
they do not want to get married in chapter 7).

Making comparisons to boys' voices through response
helps us to see even more clearly the potentially devastating
affect validating boys' voices (by hearing them in the classroom to the exclusion of the girls' voices, whether a conscious
act or not) has on girls' voices. The very genres of text and
the types of responses we "accept" (i.e., seem to value more)
applying our "critical eye" to these genres and types, further
exacerbates the inequities between boys' and girls' voices in
the classroom. How, then, do we present the types of critical
responses to texts based on models of "rigorous self-evalua-
tion," (Bigelow 1990, p. 446) social justice, peace, and feminism? How do we encourage students to not become
entrenched in providing responses formed on notions of victimization? How do we develop what Barone et al. (1995)
calls a "critical spirit," one that leads ultimately to a response
aimed at social justice and change? How do we create [new]
ways in which to validate girls' voices; how can we respond
and model response to girls so that they, too, have a voice?

Modeling a critical response is particularly difficult.
Indeed, according to Langer (1994) simply speaking the
term "response" evokes confusion and frustration from even
the "best" educators:

they are attracted to the notions underlying a pedagogy of student thoughtfulness because they think it provides students with ownership for their own learning; motivates and engages them in making sense; and provides a context for them to try out, negotiate, and refine their ideas in interaction with others. On the other hand, they are uncertain how to carry through such lessons. Often I am asked, "Does anything go, and if not, how do I know what to do? Once I get an initial response what do I do with it?"

In this study, Mr. Roscoe and myself may well have asked ourselves, "Once we get a cultural text like 'The Killer Boys,' how do we best model a critical response?"

And yet, both the boys' and Laurelei's responses to "The Killer Boys," were valid ones; responses that represented years of conditioning by society to how they viewed their particular world. In fact, it could be argued that these students simply knew no other way of viewing their own lives. But, they needed to; they needed to reconstruct their responses, to recreate them, while we needed to learn to validate all kinds of responses, finding ways, in particular, to validate the girls' responses. This reconstruction, this creation of "alternative interpretations" can lead to students' calling into question "his or her attitudes about prevailing social practices" (Barone 1995, p. 35). If continued for sustained periods of time, critical response, then, becomes, "transgressive," or:

. . . a habit of critical thinking, a spirit of curiosity that itself becomes an integral element of the plot of the student's life narrative, a significant tendency toward inquiry that becomes part of who the student is (Barone et al. 1995, p. 35).

Becoming critical in Mr. Roscoe's classroom had, indeed, helped many of the students to begin to add to their repertoire of responses in positive ways. For example, Darius' response to the words "underprivileged" and "Negro" and the girls' responses to questions of domesticity, high-

light the fact that these students were *able to* see the possi-
bility of response's role in helping to reshape their own identities. It became clear to me that even fairly well-defined
social attitudes (such as the notion that the girls must get
married and have babies) were beginning to be changed,
allowing the students to perceive themselves in increasingly
positive ways; ways outside of the traditional, negative perceptions society held of them. And although the girls still,
overall, had a difficult time as they often felt their responses
were neither "right" nor "important," they too began to
respond in small groups where they felt safe; responding
increasingly in ways that took on a critical edge. Our
responses then to them became even more crucial as we
hoped that someday, and in some ways, the girls would
move their voices and responses out of the private and into
the public sphere.

Summary

Like Lensmire (1993), I argue for a revised vision of
response in the classroom. This "re-vision," then, becomes a
complex set of responses to a complex myriad of cultural
texts and cultural stances that students create and share.
This revision assumes a modeling of critical responses by
the teacher; responses clearly tied to a larger societal discourse on social justice and change. As both teachers and
students work toward becoming critical, creating and
espousing a "critical spirit," responses become grounded in
possibilities, rather than limits, aspirations rather than
expectations, and entitlement and empowerment rather
than victimization; a victimization so often ascribed to girls'
voices.

In the next and final chapter of this book, I focus on
other curricular approaches that I believe not only provide
various opportunities for students to write and express their
voices, but also provide models from which students can
begin to question and challenge the social and cultural contexts and conditions in which they go to school and live. A

violence-prevention curriculum, for example, may be another such model as students not only read and write prolifically, but in doing so, learn to make inquiries, and search for, alternatives to violence in their schools and communities.

10

Summary, Implications, and Discussion

> Women have been in darkness for centuries. They don't know themselves. Or only poorly. And when women write, they translate this darkness . . . The writing of women is really translated from the unknown, like a new way of communicating, rather than an already formed language. (Belenky et al. 1986, p. 203)

In the classroom, writing can be used as a vehicle through which urban pre-adolescent girls can shape, construct, reconstruct, and express their voices amidst a threatening world. This was clear to me in Mr. Roscoe's fifth-grade classroom as I observed how the eleven girls used writing and talk around writing to seriously attend to the implications and consequences of their life experiences. They also used writing to challenge and to resist others' perceptions of them, experiment with others' voices, and to become active in wanting to change social conditions.

In this chapter I first explore why an expression of voice through writing is so critical for young urban girls. Second, I discuss the implications of process writing pedagogy in classrooms in general regarding this development. I then turn to a brief presentation of curricular approaches (e.g., thematic-based units) that, by design, can help us as educators attend to and allow for girls' voices in the classroom. The implications for listening to urban girls' voices, I hope, become powerfully clear. But first, I present a summary of the preceding chapters.

Summary of the Book

The purpose of this book has been to reveal the multiple voices that eleven poor, pre-adolescent girls expressed through writing in a fifth-grade urban classroom. By exploring and responding critically to these voices from within two major writing contexts, the public and the private, the girls learned not only to begin to name issues salient to them, such as domesticity and racism, but to begin to resist the underlying notions of such issues.

Following a preliminary discussion of language choice and the elusive, complex, and often contradictory nature of "voice" and its multiplicity, this study described and explained not only the contexts in which the girls wrote, but also the genres, topics, and themes they chose to use in their writing. After introductory portraits of the eleven girls themselves, this study moved toward a more concrete presentation of actual samples of voice through writing in public forums.

Next, the study turned toward an exploration of multiple voices through more private contexts, including journal writing and writers' circle. It was in these more personal writing contexts that it was shown that not only were the girls writing prolifically, but that they were also writing about issues that seemed to more truly reflect their own voices. As this inquiry progressed, both violent and productive voices emerged as the girls struggled with transforming the violent world around them into a more peaceful, productive one through activist writing stances. Finally, this study provided a brief glimpse of the boys' voices as it explored more closely the notions of cultural texts and critical response to both girls' and boys' texts.

This study has challenged the traditional notion of a process approach to writing by addressing how such an approach might become a site for significant tension and struggle over issues like ownership and voice. Multiple voices collide in this struggle as girls, in particular, search for voices of their own among the multiple voices they hear and know. This inquiry underscores the importance of including all of girls' multiple voices into the curriculum where these voices can be nurtured, cultured, and responded to in potentially productive ways.

Why an Expression of Voice?

According to Gilligan (1990), there has been a notable absence of girls in major studies. Poor urban females like the eleven girls in Mr. Roscoe's classroom have been critically underrepresented. Because the life experiences of poor, urban girls are complicated by factors of sexism, racism, and violence that affect their school experience, there is a moral imperative to explore more directly these life experiences.

The alarming dropout rate of urban females makes this examination an even more urgent one. McKenna and Ortiz (1988) report that among Latinas in public schools, 19.3% will drop out; among African-American girls in public schools, the rate is slightly lower at 14.1%. These statistics, however, may be misleading. For example, there are reports that close to 80% of all students at Northwest Elementary School who begin their education there drop out before they finish high school.

Many researchers (Fine 1991; Kozol 1991; Chicago Board of Education 1991; McKenna & Ortiz 1988; The American Association of University Women Report (AAUW) 1992) have offered various reasons for why girls leave school including pregnancy, marriage, responsibility for siblings at home, and substance abuse. In fact, the AAUW (1992) Report states that researchers continually cite pregnancy as the main reason poor, urban girls leave school. The Report claims, on the contrary, however, that,

> the commonly held belief that female students drop out because they are pregnant reflects only part of the reality: 50 to 60 percent of female dropouts report leaving school for reasons other than pregnancy (p. 48).

The Report continues by saying that "girls drop out of school simply because they do not consider school to be a pleasant or worthwhile place to spend their time" (p. 49). In other words, the stark reality may be that schools are ill-prepared and unwilling to hear and attend to girls' voices.

Fine's research (1991) supports this notion. In framing characteristics of the typical high school female drop out within an urban school, she found that moderate depression, an absence of political awareness, self-blame, low assertiveness, and high conformity led these girls to drop out of school. These girls simply had learned to shut down what Fine (1991) calls "dangerous conversations," taking these conversations and their voices out of school altogether.

The entry into adolescence makes more complex these conversations. Girls, in general, when they enter adolescence come face-to-face with a society that does not legitimize their understandings of themselves and their perspectives of their social world. Girls are "voice-trained" (Mikel-Brown & Gilligan 1993) especially by adult women who teach them when they should speak and when they should be silent. As a result, girls learn to separate their formal educational experiences from powerful learning experiences as they take their voices "underground" (Gilligan 1990). The entry into adolescence by females is intrinsically stressful; among poor, urban girls this transition may be particularly so, as race, class, and gender intersect to produce different and more pronounced patterns of stress.

The eleven girls in Mr. Roscoe's classroom began to struggle with issues related both to themselves as pre-adolescents and as poor, urban girls, expressing their own voices through various writing contexts. Both the public context of the writing workshop and other more private contexts such as our writers' circle became critically important tools in affording these girls opportunities in which to express their voices.

Process Writing: A Critical Pedagogical Tool

According to Willinsky (1990) the implementation of process writing in the classroom should reflect more than just "a desire [by the teacher] to foster an individual's story" (p. 55). Instead, it should "represent[s] a common, *critical* (emphasis added) project in the social dimensions of literature and voice that begins with the students' own situation" (p. 55). Writers' workshop, then, as the primary classroom context in which process writing is enacted, becomes:

> a literacy enfranchisement through a sort of collective sensibility and strength . . . [and through a] shared commitment and co-operative nature of the process (p. 54).

The collective sensibility that a process approach to writing fosters is the kind of that Belenky et al. (1986) believe that young girls need as "prerequisites" for learning and development (p. 194). What this means in the classroom, then, is that by implementing a process approach to writing, one is taking a stance about girls' knowledge, experiences, and voice; one is saying that they count.

Indeed, both feminist and other literacy reformists (Belenky et al. 1986; Dyson 1993; Gilligan 1990; Lensmire 1993, 1994; Willinsky 1990) talk about designing educational programs in which it is crucial to learn about "the academic experience of ordinary women" (Belenky et al. 1986, p. 190). In doing so, then, process writing, as a critical pedagogical tool, is moved to the center of the curriculum. It is here, at the center, that girls' writing becomes the "constant site of social struggle" (Willinsky 1990, p. 47). Process writing pedagogy, therefore, enacted, by the students and the teacher, has the potential to move girls' voices to the center of the classroom, reflecting at the same time the larger politics of both the classroom and the community.

This can not be accomplished, however, unless there is at the same time an effort to *respond* to the different voices and the different texts that the students create; those that are produced both within writing workshop activities and those created outside of it. Process writing, therefore, is a necessary condition for the expression of girls' voices, but not a sufficient one. The product, or "cultural text," that the girls create with their voices must also be seriously consid-

ered (See previous chapter for discussion of cultural texts)
as well as other important and innovative curricular ideas.

Curricular Implementations

A Reading-Writing, Gender-Balanced Curriculum

Girls need sufficient opportunities to engage with good
literature. Text selection is crucial to not only be held up
as role models for what the girls read and write, but also for
how they perceive themselves as "poor" and "Black/Latina"
in an urban world. Studying other "oppressed" groups
through literature, for example, can provide girls with additional role models for naming, critiquing, and resisting,
guiding them, perhaps, toward social and political meaning as a direct source of activism.

Providing girls with these opportunities is often a difficult scenario given the budget and time constraints of
urban teachers and librarians, however. Mr. Roscoe often
complained to me that it wasn't easy "getting good literature" for his students, a statement I confirmed when, after
conducting a search among his bookshelves and the
library's, I found few, if any, books written about women. I
found the standard fare: *The Double Life of Pocahantas*
(Fritz 1983), *Rosa Parks* (Greenfield 1973), and a "new"
piece, *The Class President* (Hurwitz 1990) in which the main
character, a fifth-grade girl, loses her bid for classroom president to a boy. (The boys in this classroom told me she lost,
in the end, because she was a "bitch.") In addition, there
were few, if any, books on the shelves written *by* women.
The ones I did locate might very well fall into Chantal's cat-
egory of "girly-girly" (Refer to chapter 6 for a discussion of
another one of Chantal's literature categories: "white people
and men"): *The Hand-Me-Down-Kid* (Pascal 1980) and
Seven Days to a Brand-New Me (Conford 1993) (with a ded-
ication to Robert Redford because "he knows why").

As educators we need to understand and make problematic the clear messages that are being sent to our classrooms

when literature by and about women is not included. Simply put, a lack of quality women's literature sends a strong message: women are not capable of writing quality books, nor do women have quality experiences about which to write. We need to understand how this message, then, transcends itself directly into girls' expectations of their own writing, as they see no concrete models on which to extend their voices.

Through literature, the girls can learn to see the possibilities and opportunities for social change and justice (that have been discussed in the classroom, for example) as their discussions become tied to a larger societal discourse through the very literature they are reading, writing, and responding to. Girls need to be able to see themselves and their lives through the texts that they read. Making this connection between literature and their lives, then, helps them to find models on which they can write, thereby extending their repertoire of voices.

An infusion of literature with a special emphasis on the inclusion of female-authored and female-centered literature would support the expression of girls' voices. Such a curriculum is one specifically described and promoted by the National Council of Teachers (NCTE) in *Guidelines For A Gender-Balanced Curriculum*. The guidelines clearly state that to achieve a balance, teachers need to include:

> literature by and about women [and] recognize[s] and appreciate[s] different genres (diaries, letters), different styles (spontaneous, circular), and different tones (intimate, emotional) to enhance our concept of what it is to be human (p. 2).

Connections to literature through writing can be strengthened in one other important way: making direct curricular choices through the implementation of thematic-based units.

A Thematic-Based Curriculum

A thematic-based curriculum, alternately referred to in instructional settings as: thematic units (Goodman 1986), theme cycles (Edelsky, Altwerger, Flores 1991), integrated language units (Pappas, Kiefer, & Levstik 1995), inquiry cycles (Harste, J., Short, K., & Burke, C. 1987), and theme teaching (Walmsley 1994) is one in which themes are

> developed from children's questions about the world for the instructional purpose of integrating subject areas into more cohesive, realistic, and functional units of curriculum.

In other words, both students and teachers join together in developing curriculum around a central topic of interest for a specified period of time. The inquiry itself usually extends over a semester or marking period as students write stories, plays, read books, and initiate projects, such as letter-writing campaigns, as part of the inquiry.

Thematic units often involve inquiry around broad and diverse topics that also serve to satisfy state curriculum requirements. In Mr. Roscoe's classroom, themes such as the "Solar System," "Heroes," "Movement," and "Changes" not only satisfied the state's requirements for what fifth-graders should know, but also at the same time gave the girls, in particular, initial opportunities to make inquiries and to explore issues about female heroes and human sexuality, for example, through extensive exposure to literature and writing. Mr. Roscoe had even begun to informally include issues of violence into his curriculum during class meetings or Author's Chair (1983), particularly around a sub-theme of "Changes," entitled "Careers."

According to Prothorow-Stith, a medical doctor, parent, and former surgeon general of Massachusetts, violence-prevention curricula are important avenues through which both the teacher and the students can begin to search for alternatives to violence. Although Prothorow-Stith (1991) recommends a formal program with objectives, steps, and outcomes pre-specified, a thematic unit that included an abundance of literature, writing, and response both in large and small groups to texts would help students make needed initial inquiries as they explored, defined, and perhaps, sought solutions to, the violence surrounding them.

Developing themes, therefore, can be another critical avenue in which writing and the expression of one's voice is moved toward a more prominent place in the curriculum as salient issues such as sexuality and violence can be explored.

Multiple Voices and Critical Struggles

As educators, we can provide the opportunities for the inclusion of students' diverse lived experiences and voices in our curricula. In fact, according to Bigelow (1990) it may be our moral responsibility to help students discover that their "lives are important sources of learning" as we push them to "use their stories as windows not only on their lives, but on society [as a whole]" (p. 439). Fine (1987) suggests that we work toward that goal despite the evidence she provides that educators who listen to their students' voices and include those voices into their curricula, are summarily reprimanded for introducing "extraneous materials . . . [and they] too were silenced" (p. 166).

Providing poor, urban, pre-adolescent girls like the eleven girls in Mr. Roscoe's class the opportunities to express their voices is one powerful avenue by which educators can insure that girls remain in school, rather than their searching for "alternative contexts" (Fine 1987) in which to speak and to learn. A search for alternative contexts ultimately leads many of these girls out of school altogether, where their voices on the edge of adolescence, potentially powerful, may be silenced forever.

This expression of voice has been most important in Mr. Roscoe's classroom where the eleven girls struggled, critically and in critical ways, with an expression of their voices. It is here that being able to express one's voice was a matter, quite literally, of connection and survival, where staying in school, staying involved, and believing that one's knowledge counted, was especially crucial to these girls as poor, urban, pre-adolescents.

In Mr. Roscoe's fifth-grade classroom, opportunities were clearly given for the girls to write and to express their voices within both the context of writing workshop and other contexts outside of the workshop. It was the expression of their voices that had, and will continue to have, profound effects on the choices these girls make about education in the near future. These multiple voices will continue to reflect the girls themselves—complex, often contradictory, reluctant, resistant, false, fearful, and hopeful—potentially productive, and critical, voices on the edge of adolescence.

Appendix A:
Approach and Methodology

we must [still] acknowledge that the process of translating the complexity of other people's lives and cultures into a seamless narrative takes enormous hubris. (Sheehan 1993, p. 78)

Approach

Ethnographic methodology was used in this study to investigate and describe the girls' voices through writing for three major, interrelated reasons. First, like Geertz (1973), I sought "thick description" in not only searching for the kinds of meaning that poor, urban, pre-adolescent girls had in their lives, but how they *constructed* these meanings through and by ". . . words, images, institutions, behaviors, in terms of which, in each place, people actually represent themselves to themselves and to one another" (p. 228). Second, ethnographic inquiry allowed me the opportunity to describe the girls' voices through writing in the naturalistic setting of the classroom. Such inquiry is grounded in real life and the "data of the everyday" (Belenky et al. 1986, p. 139) and provides "detailed drawings of girls' knowledge and resonant settings for girls' voices" (Gilligan 1990, p. 27). As such, ethnographic inquiry allowed me to enter into the research setting as part of the research itself. This became particularly important in this study as it has been I who has had to have been "satisfied with elusive criteria like balance, fairness, completeness, and sensitivity" within the framework of "rigorous subjectivity" inherent in ethnographic approaches (Wolcott 1991). Finally, ethnographic methodology has the potential for allowing "the interpretations of women to take center stage" (Bogdan & Biklen 1992, p. 27).

Perspective

This study has situated these urban, pre-adolescent girls' voices through writing in a larger context of feminist theory about voice, silence, reflection, and action (Belenky et al. 1986; Gilligan 1990; Hollingsworth 1992; Noddings 1992; Rogers 1993). Inherent in feminist theory is the premise that there are other intellectual capacities and experiences valued by women that do not appear in the current standard measures used to conduct research on women (Noddings 1992, p. 87). Such experiences may include, for example, oral and written text interpretation, interpersonal reasoning, production of constructive, nonadversarial responses, resistance to violence as a form of response, and managing several tasks simultaneously. Research methodologies which seek to embrace a feminist perspective, then, would include women's personal experiences as "standard," seeking to uncover and discover:

> the epistemological value of using women's experiences as resources for discovering new theory. Instead of simply validating or uncovering 'scientific truths' about mainstream cultures, feminist research asks questions that lead to changes in oppressed conditions, usually those of women, but that can also apply to men and children in underpowered life roles. (Hollingsworth 1992, p. 376)

Ethnographic research conducted from a feminist perspective aims to "address the continuing silence of [these] girls' voices in the research literature . . ." (Rogers 1993, p. 269).

Design of the Study

Setting

I had initially chosen Mr. Roscoe's classroom as a research site in April of 1991. During that time, Mr. Roscoe was transforming his classroom from what he described as a "traditional" one to a more "holistic, whole-language" classroom. Mr. Roscoe was meeting bi-monthly with other teachers from various schools across the city with a professor, Christine C. Pappas, as facilitator. The purpose of the group was not only to learn "tips" as to how to make such a transition smoothly, but also to support and encourage one another as the transition was made.

Mr. Roscoe's first major step in moving towards a more holistic classroom was to design and implement a writing process approach into his curriculum. I was particularly interested at that time in how non-native speakers of English participated in peer writing conferences and how, as a result, they made (or if they made) revisions to their written pieces.

My focus changed as I moved through my pilot study of peer writing conferences among non-native speakers as I began to notice that the girls, in particular, struggled with a perceived devalued status on much of what they had to say. This became apparent to me primarily through discussions with the girls and through their writing. Primarily, what I began to observe was a "loss of voice," a phenomenon in which the girls became increasingly silent and withdrawn as the school year progressed. I was specifically interested, then, in exploring not only what this phenomenon of a "loss of voice" was, but how it might manifest itself through the writing the girls did in the classroom.

Participants

Twenty-eight students and I shared Mr. Roscoe's classroom during the 1992–1993 academic school year. Of the total twenty-eight, only eleven were female while seventeen were males. The predominant cultural/linguistic group was Latino, with twenty-two students in all. The primary participants in this study were the eleven pre-adolescent girls. Eight were Latina; two African-American; and one Angla, who was also considered to be hearing and "language" impaired. All but two of the girls were ten years old at the time of this study, the remaining two were eleven years old. All but three of the girls had started their schooling at Near Northwest; Mr. Roscoe reported that he had had two of the girls several years before in Kindergarten. All of the eleven girls participated with me in writers' circle. All of the eleven girls shared writing with me, including pieces for Author's Chair, journal writing, and even writing from previous years.

Procedures

Rationale

It has been both through the common and uncommon experiences these girls and I shared that I placed myself as a "research instrument" firmly within the context of this study, believing that the:

> self is a researcher's finest and most valuable touchstone for making relationships and creating interpretations throughout the research process. (Rogers 1993, 267)

Nested within this research process is the notion of a voice-centered, relational approach (Rogers 1993). The practice of this research entails that the researcher is:

> listening to girls and women as authorities about their own experiences and representing their voices in a written text, rather than replacing their words with psychological interpretations that cannot be questioned by the reader. Listening to girls and women in this way requires us to bring ourselves into relationship with another subjective voice . . . (p. 267)

I first began this study with a firm belief that this research was being conducted for not only purposeful ends, but also for caring and responsive ends (Noddings 1992). I had no idea, however, what was entailed by "caring and responsive ends." It was only through my work with these girls that I learned how truly little these eleven girls had been listened to and how, after some time, they would come to cherish the opportunities we had together to speak our minds. It was only through my growing relationships with them that I realized the overwhelming significance of my role in their lives, and theirs in mine. Putting oneself "into relationship with another subjective voice" is an extremely riskful and frightening experience. (This became painfully obvious when, one month into the new academic year, Laurelei called me in tears, to tell me her life was back to a point where "no one listened, no one cares.") It is also an experience, however, that, when "accomplished," is an incredibly rewarding one.

Accomplishing the task of coming into relationship with the eleven girls in Mr. Roscoe's classroom was one that needed to be carefully planned and nurtured. Primarily, I needed to build into my procedures a way in which the girls and I could share our writing and ourselves in a safe, non-threatening way. For these reasons, I began "writers' circle," the group in which I and the eleven girls, through writing, grew to know each other better throughout the year.

General Procedures

For the present study, I gathered observational data 2 days per week for the entire academic year of 1992–1993. In September of 1992, I spent most of my observational time familiarizing myself with the "new" group of fifth-grade students in Mr. Roscoe's classroom. During the remaining months of 1992, October through December, I attempted to establish an "insider's view" (Wolcott 1990, 1992) of the classroom, as I moved to establish rapport specifically with the 11 girls in Mr. Roscoe's classroom. As I transcribed audiotapes, photocopied artifacts, and typed fieldnotes, I began to "funnel" (Spradley 1980) the data in order to get a sense of the whole picture and of what happened where, when, and with whom.

In December of 1992, I narrowed my scope, intensifying my study of specific events, settings, and people to reconceptualize the notion of voice. In doing this, I set up a writing context called "writers' circle" in which the girls and I wrote and shared our ideas about writing.

Writers' Circle Procedures

Just before Christmas recess, I began to explain to the girls what I envisioned writers' circle to be and to ask them if they would like to participate. I explained that I was particularly interested in what they had to say through writing, how they chose topics and genres, to whom they wrote, and for what purposes. I also explained to them that, eventually, I would like to use their writing to write about their lives. They all agreed and Mr. Roscoe and I wrote and sent home permission forms in both Spanish and English. (All but Alejandra's mother approved of our group. When asked, we learned from Alejandra that her father had actually signed the form saying that she could not participate because there were family problems at home. At Alejandra's insistence, her mother finally sent in her written permission for Alejandra to participate.) Mr. Roscoe and I decided that it was best to split the girls into two groups for our meetings for two major reasons. First, we had to meet at the end of the hallway near Mr. Roscoe's door and the stairwell and there was little room for five or six of us, let alone eleven. In addition, Mr. Roscoe's students had a heavy pull-out schedule that included science, gym, art, and bilingual classes. It was, for example, because of the all-morning bilingual pull-out program that Teresa, Cynthia, Alejandra, and Yolanda participated in, that they were chosen to become part of the afternoon writers' circle group. Initially we met each group twice a week. Because of ever-changing schedules in the school, however, sometimes I met with each group only one time per week. We met from January until June of the academic year.

At our first meeting of writers' circle, I gave each girl a journal and decided on some general rules to guide us through these meetings. The first rule was that we would brainstorm topics on which to write and that the girls could write any additional pieces they wanted to. The second rule was that the journals were private. That is, no one could be forced to share something she did not want to. And the third rule was that no "swear words" would be allowed. We decided that we could learn to say what we needed to say without the use of swear words.

Interestingly, by spring each of our initial rules was broken. For example, the girls became so interested in writing on what they wanted that we stopped brainstorming on topics. Second, some of the journals were stolen or lost by the girls, effectively quelching any notion of privacy the girls felt. (Actually, the girls said they were used to having no privacy.) And third, even though most of the girls did their best to omit swear words from their writing, sometimes it became impossible. I then used those incidents to explain the uses and origins of certain vulgar words, and we compared the meanings to similar words in Spanish.

Lucy, perhaps, describes best what Writers' Circle meant to the girls:

> The Brett Club is something that just girls do or want to we can talk about anything we want to talk about. We tell Brett want [what] happens to us or want we want to happen. We tell her stuff like girls' stuff she does not tell Mr. Roscoe or no other teacher's Sometimes we write, look and read book's and magizen's like: YM [Young & Modern], Seventeen, Bazar, and other magizen's No Men no boys. Just US Girls.

Toward the end of the year, I reminded the girls that I would like to use their writing to write about their lives and we subsequently spend quite a bit of time choosing suitable nicknames for them.

Data Analysis

Wolcott (1992) claims that one of the strengths of ethnographic methodology is its potential to contribute to the field using its methods for data analysis. Because voice through writing among poor, urban girls has gone particularly unnoticed in the educational research, the analysis here took on a critical role.

Like Brown & Gilligan (1992), I had to, however, in anticipating analyzing my data, build into my design "the space for a woman or girl to speak in her own voice" (p. 22). That is, I had to relinquish the idea of a clearly-delineated analysis schema for one which, "messy and unpredictable" (p.) more accurately and honestly reflected the girls' voices through writing.

With this in mind, tapes were transcribed, and fieldnotes were typed, after each day in Mr. Roscoe's classroom. I also included my notes on the girls' perceptions, non-verbal communications, perspectives, and emotions that were not captured by the tapes or fieldnotes alone. It was crucial as well, that I added *my* perceptions, perspectives, and emotions as my subjective role was an integral component of the research process.

I next constructed a set of categories that seemed to best describe the kinds of writing and the kinds of contexts in which the eleven girls were actually doing writing. To make sense of the data I collected, I first grouped together the data under eight very general thematic categories that included "reading-writing connections" and "process writing and the diverse learner." These tentative, "messy" categories then allowed me to sift through the girls' writing and literally funnel their texts into two much more specific categories: public writing and private writing. From a public and private writing stance, then, I was able to capture the multiplicity of the girls' voices as they wrote for different audiences.

I, like Rogers (1993) have not set out to "test hypotheses about human development" (p. 269), so that certain theoretical constructs do not, and can not, reveal and reflect that which I attempted to capture through a voice-centered, relational approach. Similar to the notion of "triangulation" (Eisner 1991, p. 110), however, I offer structural corroboration as the primary means by which my perspectives here may be judged valid.

Structural corroboration (Eisner 1991) refers to the structuring of the evidence so that the researcher is concerned with three important, interrelated considerations (Hawthorne 1992, 139–140). These are:

1. Do the pieces fit together into a coherent whole?
2. Are the pieces mutually supportive?
3. Is the research "believable?"

The validity of the research, then, becomes an "interactive assessment" (p. 141) between the researcher and the readers.

In making claims to the generalizability of this study, I turn both to Eisner (1985) and feminist relational theory (Brown & Gilligan, Belenky, Rogers). First, Rogers (1993) dismisses generalizability altogether, offering "usefulness" as the measure by which a study like mine should be considered. Eisner (1985), on the other hand, offers "naturalistic" generalizations, or "perspectives as opposed to propositions," where "themes" illuminate educators' decisions and interpretations in the classroom. Both theories are useful and illuminating here.

Summary

Ethnographic methodology requires compromise and the ability to refine data that is often messy and unpredictable. Ethnographic methodology from a feminist perspective requires that these comprises are not in the form of silencing girls' voices further, but rather seeks to represent their voices as honestly and naturally as possible.

There are lessons to be learned from listening to girls' and women's voices (Belenky et al. 1986), lessons that cannot be garnered from research methodologies in which girls' voices are reduced to numerical or statistical representations. Ethnographic methodology has allowed me to offer here perspectives rather than definitive conclusions; possibilities, rather than probabilities; to share rather than to prove.

Appendix B:
The Ethics of "Doing"
Ethnographic Research

If we recognize race, class, gender and sexuality to be socially and historically contingent, then silence, retreat, and engagement all pose ethical dilemmas. All are tangled within the ethics of knowing, writing, and acting. (Fine 1994, p. 81)

Ethnography from a feminist perspective affords girls and women (and other underrepresented groups) the space within which to speak as their voices are able to "take center stage" (Bogdan & Biklen 1992) and particular ethnographic methods help the researcher to create the space in which to represent those voices in clear and convincing ways. One of the primary methods used by ethnographers to become "close" to the people they are observing and working among, is participant observation (Spradley 1980). Participant observation is described by anthropologists to be one whereby, "an outsider becomes an insider, a stranger becomes a friend, and confidences become data . . ." (Brettell 1993, p. 110).

In my first encounters with the girls in Mr. Roscoe's class, I was indeed most concerned with attaining insider status with them. Initial major questions for me, then, were: How do I become an insider among these girls, and if/when I do, how could I as an (former?) outsider possibly understand? Do I then become an insider and outsider simultaneously?

Later, as I became more comfortable in my role as participant observer, and as the girls talked and wrote more and more about their lives in our writers' circle, shifting my status among them to that of insider, I began to ask myself "new" questions such as: Was I making the girls the "Other" and how was this notion of the "Other" being mediated between us? For example, was my position as a white, middle-class woman alone enough to situate the girls as the "Other," as it placed me, perhaps, comfortably in a "lofty" position of compassion and decency for the "Other?" Will they accept, therefore, and appreciate how I present their voices? Does my writing resonate with their voices? Could I and *would I* accurately and honestly represent their voices? How could my writing express their voices while keeping them safe and maintaining their sense of privacy? What, then, *was* safe to write?

The purpose of this appendix chapter is first to pose particular questions around the ethics of "doing" ethnographic research and the ethics of response. These questions center around issues of disclosure, confidence, and safety, while at the same time addressing underlying ethical tensions such as insider/outsider status and the notion of the "Other." Second, I will review some of the current research that helps to elucidate an exploration of these questions, and third, I will highlight (by using student samples) how I attended to particular ethical questions and tensions around writing, response, and voice in Mr. Roscoe's classroom. Finally, I will outline what I believe are further questions around which continued discussion needs to take place. I hope by doing so I will contribute to a much-needed dialogue around the ethical issues I have raised here.

The Ethics of Ethnography: Guidelines for the Field

It is important here to reiterate certain points I have discussed in previous chapters, as well as to offer new, perhaps broader perspectives on the ethics of ethnography. Following are three "guidelines" that helped to frame and support more clearly these new perspectives as well as the struggles I faced surrounding various ethical tensions and dilemmas in Mr. Roscoe's classroom.

First, it is the researchers who need "to appreciate the ethical nuances associated with different research methods and different research contexts" (Howe & Dougherty 1993, p. 16). Ethnography, by design, places ethical questions and dilemmas at its forefront because it necessarily dwells on "issues of complexity" like ethical ones, including, for example, features of intimacy and open-endedness (Peshkin 1993, p. 28). Indeed, it is because of the potential of intimacy, [that ethnographic inquiry is] "more ethically charged and unpredictable from the onset . . . [and that] the 'ethical waters' are muddied" (Howe & Dougherty 1993, pp. 18–19).

Second, then, this knowledge, or anticipation, of "muddying the waters," bears heavily on one's initial research decisions. In other words, as the researcher is making choices among methodological approaches, she needs to be making a judgment, an *ethical* judgment, about what kinds of outcomes are possible, and how then those potential, perhaps intimate and open-ended, outcomes can best be represented. Finally, therefore, ethnographic inquiry "*necessitates* (emphasis mine) a judgment that leads [one] to decide what research design [one] should frame to produce . . . desirable outcomes" (Peshkin 1993, p. 23). Here, those "outcomes" initially centered around confidence, disclosure and safety; outcomes that indeed had strong ethical undertones as I struggled to represent poor, urban girls' voices clearly and honestly through their own writing.

The Ethics of Disclosure: Samples from the Field

The ethical tensions around confidence and disclosure were, for me, initially mediated by the girls' own declarations that saying what they wanted "didn't matter" because "no one listened anyhow" and if they did, "no one would care." So, even as I took these statements to be "true," i.e., I recorded and reported their words, it, too, at the same time, seemed quite peculiar to me particularly since the girls rarely (if ever) shared any of their writing in the public contexts of the classroom. In other words, I guessed they must care, they must have some sense that what they wrote and/or talked about could "embarrass" them, or worse could actually "hurt" them in some way. How, then, I thought could I make ethnographically meaningful connections between "publicly and privately available information" (Jaffe 1993, p. 80) while at the same time maintaining a level of trust and confidence among the girls themselves?

This ethical tension was particularly salient during my numerous conversations with Laurelei. (Remember, Laurelei was one of the more vocal girls in Mr. Roscoe's classroom who expressed a persistent displeasure that no one, including her parents and Mr. Roscoe listened to her.) In these many conversations with her, in fact, Laurelei reiterated her unhappiness vis-à-vis adults, while insisting that I not "tell" the adults that she felt that way. Here is an excerpt from a conversation we had about why she didn't like Mr. Roscoe and the classroom (See chapter 4 for another excerpt of a similar conversation); an ongoing conversation whose larger theme was most always one of unfairness and an unwillingness to listen.

LAURELEI: You won't tell Mr. Roscoe?

BRETT: No!

LAURELEI: For real?

BRETT: For real.

LAURELEI: Ok. Because I don't like Mr. Roscoe that much.

BRETT: Ok. That's fair. Any particular reason?

LAURELEI: Because he's not fair.

BRETT: Because he's not fair, why . . . why?

LAURELEI: Because there's a lot of things he's done and they're not fair, and he makes me angry and everything.

BRETT: Can you give me an example?

LAURELEI: No, just because he's not fair, that's it.

Since I share the belief that we are "never wholly other" from those we study (Jaffe 1993, p. 52), making decisions whether to disclose in the name of research, to disclose in the interest of "one being heard," or not to disclose at all, for example, became, often, like a circus act: the delicate balance of a tightrope walker, moving back and forth, carefully, sometimes with confidence, other times tentatively and with trepidation and/or regret, not knowing when one was "inside" or "outside" or, ultimately, when one might fall, having completely overstepped and misjudged ethical boundaries and spaces altogether.

Repeating Laurelei's words (albeit not directly to Mr. Roscoe) seems now to be one of those missteps, even as it was caught and cushioned with rationales and justifications that included most prominently the statement that I "owed" it to "others" that Laurelei's voice be heard.

The Ethics of Response: Samples from the Field

Laurelei's conversations reminded me, in retrospect, that there were many times, however, that I felt "wholly other" from the girls; a tension I constantly struggled with. In the classroom, this tension manifested itself in broader contexts, too, as I wrestled with the idea that as I responded to the girls, I really only could respond with respect to our status as females. That is, in crucial ways our differences (e.g., linguistically and racially) for example, were historically and socially constructed, and firmly entrenched, to force us to maintain a distance; to necessitate that I stand on the "outside" gazing inward at the "Other." This construction was further exacerbated by the fact that the girls considered themselves the "Other" (evidenced by statements such as Walinda's that they were, indeed, poor and Black because there was no nurse on staff at the school); a notion that was reinforced daily by society via the media, and even other teachers and the girls' own families.

At the same time, though, it became apparent that through our struggles and our explorations of gender and race, that we were (albeit perhaps in "small" ways) making problematic our status as women situated within *different* socio/historical/cultural contexts. And it was the explicit exploration of our statuses within these broader contexts too that I began to understand that I could not construct an unproblematic "Other" without making the self problematic; a necessary struggle Fine (1994) describes as "working the hypen" (i.e., "self-Other") in an attempt to "reconcile the slippery constructions of self and "Other" [and] rendering those constructions "fluid" rather than "fixed" (p. 78).

In Mr. Roscoe's classroom the manifestation of this interplay between the self and the "Other" was most clearly visible in the kinds of stories the girls told, but also in their responses, and ultimately, in both my responses to their voices and my decision(s) to disclose, and make public, those responses. In responding, the ethical tensions often became much more clear—and much more dramatic—leading to a further set of questions, layered more deeply and complexly in the larger framework of ethnographic research.

Response, by definition, sets up different ethical tensions around issues of privacy and disclosure. Primarily, if one follows that *response is the meaning* (Fish 1980, p.3) and that meaning can only be enacted if there is "answerability" (Bakhtin 1981; 1986) (i.e., authors and audiences responding to each other outside of the text in ways negotiated and understood by both parties) then response becomes a necessary component of mediating the tension between the ethnographer and the "Other," for example. That is, responding and taking a position is "an ethical imperative" (Jaffe 1993, p. 56) in becoming self-critical and making problematic the "Other."

The other major theme in Laurelei's texts and conversations—adults' unwillingness to listen—helps to highlight, rather dramatically, this "ethical imperative" for response. Originally presented in chapter 7, I present it here again:

> My mother's cuison She's 15 she wen't out with a man but she didn't have a baby because she use condoms. and

she still told her mother she did it. she was dem she
shouldn't told her mother because she didn't get pregnant
and her mother hit her and then she wen't to her room
and try to kill herself the ambulance came her mother is
my mothers ant by my mother's mom and I don't know no
more!

Responding to Laurelei's concerns led to many conversations with her and the other girls in writers' circle
about their own sexuality, including having their periods,
condoms and condom use, and both sexual and non-sex-
ual relationships. (My responses often centered around
helping the girls to see that there were, indeed, adults
who could be turned to for advice without fear of physical
and/or emotional reprisals.) And yet, too, as extremely difficult and sensitive issues arose, such as the cultural
taboos around acceptable sexual and sexually-related
behavior for young girls, I had to examine *myself*; my
beliefs and my responses to those beliefs much more
closely. Through response, I was able to better examine
who I was within broader, culturally-constructed contexts
and boundaries.

Issues of deciding what and how to represent the girls'
voices, then, increasingly became ones of confidence, disclosure, and safety; rendered even more salient as I was made
increasingly privy to private feelings and conversations and
asked to respond to them. One of the most frightening and
urgent decisions around disclosure and response centered
around Jane's family life (see chapter 7). She had initiated
an exchange of notes with me to inform me her "family was
falling apart," demanding a reply from me—evident in such
statements as, "it was *your* turn to write back." Because
Jane herself had sought an urgent response from me, I
believed that it was my obligation to provide such a
response. (The exchange began after Jane had written the
piece entitled, "Unfair" about her father moving out. For
emphasis and easy reference, I reproduce that first piece,
originally found in chapter 4, and her series of notes, originally found in chapter 7, again here):

Unfair

The thing that unfare to me is that my Dad had to move
out. I don't like it. The reason why is because? I think that
this is not fair. I am traing [trying] my best to get ous [us]
back togather but it is not working. This is hurting my
mom bcasue we dont tock [talk] to her that much. And I
think my mom like some one os [else]. He allways come
over and sade Hi. And I dont like it not one bit. I think that
my mom is doing the rong [wrong] thing because it is hurd
[hurting] all of ous. And my flamey [family] is folling apart.

When Jane wrote this first piece "Unfair" in her journal
for writers' circle (based on a themed assignment the girls
themselves had chosen), the group talked about divorce,
families moving away and apart, and "blame." Many girls
shared similar stories (remember Nayda's story about her
father moving out of state, for example) and even I was able
to talk about my own experiences as a now single parent of
a young son; the guilt and blame I often felt, and my own
fears around living in a large city alone with a child. The following note, stirring, yet realistic, underscores and gives
testimony to the fact that Jane, nor any one of us was alone:

Dear Nayda:

I'm sorry about your father. I wish you were with him. I
[one] can't support children with out there father or
mother. I'm sorry about dat [that]. I'm sorry very sorry.
I'm sorry about it. I like your story. Maribel

It seemed, then, that it was *because of* the "safe" spaces
provided in writers' circle that Jane and the other girls
gained the sense that they were not alone and could continue to write about family situations, without judgment
nor reprisal. Jane's audience, however, changed when she
began writing me notes and letters exclusively—leading her
away from the known shared contexts and supports of the
writers' circle group, to a lesser-known, perhaps, *assumed*
supportive one in me. (Lacking my written replies to Jane's
notes—I had given them to her and had not "in the name of

research" thought to copy such private letters. I can only here reconstruct [from my fieldnotes] the kinds of responses I made to Jane's letters):

> Dear Brett:
>
> I have to talk to some one But I don't know how I wont [want] to talk to you But I don't know if you will undreside [understand].

In this first note (above), as Jane entered unfamiliar territory, she carefully and tentatively sought out my reaction (and interest) by framing her "problems" as ones that I may not understand. When I replied simply, "tell me more, I can only help if you tell me what's going on," she became more bold; even thankful that I had bothered to write back. Her second note, where she informed me that her uncle had just died compelled me, however, without her knowledge, to go to Mr. Roscoe before I attempted to write her back:

> Thank you for the note what I was tonking [talking] about is I can ut those suf [stuff] in my Direy and you are the only one to read it. My moms bother [brother] just die and her borther girl frind going to die that why we are moving and I roit [write] you.

Interestingly (I had remembered thinking) Mr. Roscoe was privy to this fact already and it was he who informed me that her uncle had died of AIDS, as had other students' family members in the classroom. Seeming not too concerned, then, that this was a particularly uncommon occurrence, nor a particularly urgent one, I replied how sorry I was and asked her if she wanted to talk further about it. I went on to recount stories of how I often missed family members, including a detailed one about my son who was on vacation with his grandparents.

The following week, Jane delivered to me this note:

> Dear Brett
>
> Hi It was your turn to write me Did you son come back [from vacation] I know my dad dind't I don't think I should

tell you anything anymore Iam aforad [afraid] that he will
find out. he wont if you Don't tell him I don't know what I
should do I have to talk to some one so I could let all this
out. It is just bilding up more and more. I dont know why I
write like this I have it I like to writ like this Write back.

It was Jane's final note to me about her family and it stirred
profound guilt feelings from me, including the sense that
perhaps I had not been attentive enough, e.g., "it was your
turn to write back . . . I don't know what I should do I have
to talk to someone . . .", nor helpful enough in providing a
safe context in which to speak, nor, perhaps finally, in giving
her concrete solutions on how to handle her feelings. I felt I
hadn't fully (nor quickly enough) understood the gravity of
the situation, especially as it related to Jane's overall self-
esteem and well-being. And I regretted not having made
more convincing and honest attempts to be a genuine support, rather than going to (running to?) Mr. Roscoe, leaving the onus of the problem to fall on his shoulders. Once
again, as tightrope walker, I had fallen, misjudging the ethical waters altogether.

And yet, how could I have responded in ways that Jane
would have accepted and used to better understand and to
cope with her situation? Is an ethical dilemma present in a
response or in lack of response? And what are/should have
been my responsibilities to those responses or lack of
responses?

Alvermann (1993) tells us that to *not* respond is uneth-
ical; Lensmire (1993) reminds us that in any utterance or
response we make to students, "ethical and political issues
are at stake" (p. 281); Fine (1987) adds that to ". . . *not* name
[nor respond] . . . [is] a particular form of silencing; whereas
Bigelow (1990) insists that the only "justifiable response . . .
is [one that will] equip students to understand and critique
the society in which they live" (p. 437). So, as much as a
sense of well-being and responsibility toward the girls
became important to me in my responding, I understood,
too, that my *lack* of responding served to do little to equip
the girls to begin to name and critique the injustices they

were faced with, furthering silencing their voices altogether. This became painfully clear in my lack of response toward the boys' stories, especially ones like "Killer Boys" that were replete with dangerously violent and sexist language.

A Justification of Ethics: The Heart of Morality

Previously in chapter 9, I wrote about my perceived need for both students and the teacher(s) to become rigorously self-critical and reflective. This rigor was necessary, I explained, so that one could not only begin to learn to challenge racist and sexist assumptions that pervade one's own cultural stances, but also to begin to learn to *respond* to those assumptions in critical ways; a process Lensmire (1993) described as examining, critically, the "traditionally given" (p. 275). I wrote, too however, about the *lack of response* from both Mr. Roscoe and myself, particularly during an Author's Chair reading of, "The Killer Boys." (The story is reprinted again here):

Killer Boys

It was some boys that they thought they were bad, they were 21 years old. So evey time some one would look at them and they would kill them. So one time a cop tryed to get one of the killer boys. So the cop shot him, he shot him in the leg so two of the killer boys came and killed the cop, two of the killer boys came and took the one that got shot to the hospital. So one time a old ladie looked at them and they killed the old ladie . . . So [we] took out a gun so we left to our car and got some guns then we waited in it till they came, a old ladie came out of the alley and they raipt her and killed her, so I went over and they throw the old ladie in a garbage can . . . then we went to our limo and we went to pack up the babes and we went to are castle and we went to sleep with them in the badroom, the names of the girl's were . . .

Although I was virtually silent during the students' reading and response to this piece, listening to this story pushed me to explore much more seriously and deeply the foundations of a renewed framework for many of the ethical dilemmas, and ultimately, the ethical decisions (e.g., of disclosure) I needed to make in Mr. Roscoe's classroom. Central to this renewed framework initially, however, were rationales and justifications, and as they began to take shape and be heard, they were increasingly fueled and perpetuated by the very ethical tensions they were meant to explain and diffuse.

For example, in both my responses to the girls' writing and my lack of response to the portrayal of women in stories like "Killer Boys," came justifications, many quite contradictory. They included: "their voices need to be heard," "I can be their spokesperson," (what if there weren't a 'Brett'), "it was better ignored or left unsaid," "it was only fantasy," and "I didn't know what to say, and didn't want to say something wrong." The reality of such contrary rationales forced me to sort out and to reexamine, once again, what my role was, from an ethical standpoint, vis-à-vis Mr. Roscoe's students.

Essentially, examining where such justifications may have fit within an ethical framework helped me to see that I no longer needed to spend my time rationalizing and defending my responses nor my lack of responses to the students' writing, realizing finally, that "the search for justification often carries us farther and farther from the heart of morality" (Noddings 1984, p. 105). In other words, I had to confront any ethical, pedagogical, and political dilemmas fully cognizant that in doing so, I would find *profound contradictions* and that it was within those profound contradictions that, indeed, ethical questions would "boil" (Fine 1994, p. 80). I needed to respond, to take a stance, and to critically examine both myself, my assumptions, and those of the girls with whom I worked, working to:

> engage narratives written against Othering, analyzing not just the decontextualized voices of Others, but the very structures, ideologies, contexts, and practices that constitute Othering. (Fine 1994, p. 70)

It had simply become too personal and too political to do otherwise.

"Working the Hypens." Conversations for the Future

"Distance is . . . ethnographic fiction (Jaffe, p. 51) so that learning about the extremely delicate balance between involvement/detachment and disclosure/response has great ethical implications. We as ethnographers need to recognize that our work will always "stand in some relation to Othering" (Fine, p. 74) and we, therefore, need to accept the fact that the self and the "Other" are "knottily entangled" (p. 72). This acceptance, becomes a respect, then, not a defense of the integrity of one's work and one's ethics. It also becomes a "social struggle[s] with those who have been exploited" (Fine 1994). It is in this way that our work as ethnographers forces us to constantly work "the hypen" between the self and the "Other."

Critical discussions need to continue around the ethics of "doing" classroom-based ethnography. Primarily, it seems to me that there remains several issues that could fuel such a discussion, including questions like, "What do we do when they [participants] read what we have written?," or "What if they want to "lead unexamined lives"— do they have "the right *not* to be analyzed?" Yet, more importantly, the critical issue may lie in our abilities to question *ourselves* as we re-explore the ethical framework upon which and from which we conduct our work, addressing and confronting the profound contradictions inherent in our work, as we explicitly acknowledge that all our work is political. I believe we must understand that ethical tensions and dilemmas are "never resolved in the neutral or by not getting involved," (Fine 1994, p. 76), and exuberantly put the "struggle back into our texts" (Fine 1994, p. 71) so that we can work toward social justice and change. Only then do we truly "work the hypens" and bring ourselves and our work closer to the "heart of morality."

Summary

This appendix chapter has posed questions around the ethics of conducting ethnographic research, including the ethics of response in the classroom. In exploring the, all-too-often-stated dichotomous notions of insider/outsider and self/Other, while struggling with issues of disclosure, confidence, and safety, ethnographers find "profound contradictions" in their work. Yet, it is only by acknowledging these profound contradictions that the work of the ethnographer truly becomes a work closely associated with and "knottingly entangled" by conceptions of morality.

References

Altieri, J. (1994, December). *An examination of multiethnic readers' preference for literature portraying diverse cultures.* Paper presented at the annual National Reading Conference, San Diego, CA.

Alvermann, D. (1993). Student voice in class discussion: A feminist poststructuralist perspective. *Paper presented at the National Reading Conference.* Charleston, SC.

Ammon, P. (1985). Helping children learn to write in English as a second language: Some observations and hypotheses. In S.W. Freedman (Ed.), *The acquisition of written language* (pp. 65–84). Norwood, NJ: Ablex.

Ang, I. (1992). Melodramatic identifications: Television, fiction, and women's fantasy. In Brown, M.E. (Ed.), *Television and Women's Culture* (pp. 75–88). Newbury Park, CA: Sage.

Atwell, N. (1987). *In the middle: Writing, reading, and learning with adolescents.* Portsmouth, NH: Heinemann.

Bakhtin, M. (1986). *Speech genres and other late essays.* Austin: University of Texas Press.

Bakhtin, M. (1981). *The dialogic imagination.* Austin: University of Texas Press.

Bambara, T.C. (1980). What it is I think I'm doing anyhow. In Sternburg, J. (Ed.), *The writer on her work: Contemporary women writers reflect on their art and situation* (pp. 153–168). New York: W.W. Norton.

Barnett, R. C., Biener, L. & Baruch, G.K. (1987). (Eds.). *Gender and stress.* New York, NY: The Free Press.

Barton, J. (1994, December). *The influence of culturally based literature instruction on reader stance: Grade 4.* Paper presented at the annual National Reading Conference, San Diego, CA.

Bateson, M.C. (1990). *Composing a life.* New York, NY: The Penguin Group.

Beach, R. (1994a, December). *High school students' responses to portrayal of racial discrimination in short stories.* Paper presented at the annual National Reading Conference, San Diego, CA.

Beach, R. (1994b, December). *Research on stance and response to literature.* Paper presented at the annual National Reading Conference, San Diego, CA.

Beach, R., & Hynds, S. (1991). Research on response to literature. In R. Barr, M. Kamil, P. Mosenthal, & P. Pearson, (Eds.), *Handbook of reading research II* (pp. 453–489). NY: Longman.

Beach, R., & Wendler, L. (1987). Developmental differences in response to a story. *Research in the Teaching of English, 21,* 286–297.

Belenky, M.F., Clinchy, B.M, Goldberger, N.R., & Tarule, J.M. (1986). *Women's ways of knowing: The development of self, voice, and mind.* New York: Basic Books.

Bell, L. A. (1991). Changing our ideas about ourselves: Group consciousness raising with elementary school girls as a means to empowerment. In C.E. Sleeter (Ed.), *Empowerment through multicultural education* (pp. 229–249). Albany: State University of New York Press.

Best, R. (1983). *We've all got scars: What boys and girls learn in elementary schools.* Bloomington, IN: Indiana University Press.

Bigelow, W. (1990). Inside the classroom: Social vision and critical pedagogy. *Teachers College Record 91:*437–448.

Blair, C.P. (1988). Only one of the voices: Dialogic writing across the curriculum. *College English 50:*383–389.

Blake, B.E. (August 1995). Broken silences: Writing and the construction of 'cultural texts' by urban, pre-adolescent girls. *Journal of Educational Thought.*

Blake, B.E. (1992). Talk in non-native and native English speakers' peer writing conferences: What's the difference? *Language Arts* 69:604–610.

Blake, R. (1989). Explorations and new directions for teaching literature: An introduction. In R. Blake (Ed.), *Reading, writing, and interpreting literature* (pp. vi–xxiii). Schenectady, NY: New York State English Council.

Bogdan, R.C. & Biklen, S.K. (1992). *Qualitative research for education: An introduction to theory and methods*. Needham Heights, MA: Allyn and Bacon.

Brettell, C.B. (1993). Introduction: Fieldwork, text, and audience: In C.B. Brettell (Ed.), *When they read what we write: The politics of ethnography* (pp. 1–24). Westport, CT: Bergin & Garvey.

Brown, L.M. & Gilligan, C. (1992). *Meeting at the crossroads: Women's psychology and girls' development*. Cambridge, MA: Harvard University Press.

Bruner, J. (1986). *Actual minds, possible worlds*. Cambridge, MA: Harvard University Press.

Burke-LeFevre, K. (1987). *Invention as a social act*. Carbondale, IL: Southern Illinois Press.

Bush, D.M. & Simmons, R. (1987). Gender and coping with the entry into early adolescence. In Barnett, R.C., Biener, L., & Baruch, G.K. (Eds.), *Gender and stress* (pp.185–217). New York, NY: The Free Press/Macmillan.

Calkins, L.M. (1986). *The art of teaching writing*. Portsmouth, NH: Heinemann.

Calkins, L.M. (1983). *Lessons from a child*. Portsmouth, NH: Heinemann.

Carson, J.E., Carrell, P.L., Silberstein, S. Kroll, B., & Kuehn, P.A. (1990). Reading-writing relationships in first and second language. *TESOL Quarterly* 24:245–266.

Cazden, C. (1988). *Classroom discourse: The language of teaching and learning*. Portsmouth, NH: Heinemann.

Chicago Board of Education, Research and Evaluation. (March 1991). *High school dropout profile: A trend report on the graduating classes of 1982–1990*. Chicago: Chicago Board of Education.

Cisneros, S. (1989). *The house on Mango Street.* New York: Vintage Books.

Crowley, S. (1989). *A teacher's introduction to deconstruction.* Urbana, IL: NCTE.

Cummins, J. (1986). Empowering minority students: A framework for intervention. *Harvard Educational Review 56*:18–36.

Delpit, L.D. (1988). The silenced dialogue: Power and pedagogy in educating other people's children. *Harvard Educational Review 58*:84–102.

Delpit, L.D. (1986). Skills and other dilemmas of a progressive Black educator. *Harvard Educational Review 56*:379–385.

Dyson, A.H. (1995). The courage to write: Child meaning making in a contested world. *Language Arts 72*:324–333.

Dyson, A.H. (1993). *Social worlds of children learning to write in an urban primary school.* New York: Teachers College Press.

Dyson, A.H. (1992). Whistle for Willie, lost puppies, and cartoon dogs: The sociocultural dimensions of young children's composing. *Journal of Reading Behavior XXIV*:433–462.

Dyson, A.H. (1991). Viewpoints: The word and the world-reconceptualizing written language development or do rainbows mean a lot to little girls? *Research in the Teaching of English 25*:97–123.

Dyson, A.H. (1990). Research currents: Diversity, social responsibility, and the story of literacy. *Language Arts 67*:192, 206.

Dyson, A.H. & Freedman, S.W. (1990). On teaching writing: A review of the literature. *Occasional Paper No. 20,* Berkeley, CA: Center for the Study of Writing.

Dyson, A.H. (1988). Negotiating among multiple worlds: The space/time dimensions of young children's composing. *Research in the Teaching of English 22*:355–390.

Dyson, A. H. (1984). Learning to write/learning to do school: Emergent writers' interpretations of school literacy tasks. *Research in the Teaching of English 18*:233–264.

Edelsky, C., Alwerger, B., & Flores, B. (1991). *Whole language: What's the difference?* Portsmouth, NH: Heinemann.

Edelsky, C. & Hudelson, S. (1989). Contextual complexities: Written language policies for bilingual programs. *Occasional Paper No. 10*. Berkeley, CA: Center for the Study of Writing.

Edelsky, C. (1982). Writing in a bilingual program: The relation of L1 and L2 texts. *TESOL Quarterly 16*:211–228.

Eisner, E. (1991). *The enlightened eye*. New York, NY: Macmillan.

Ellis, J. (1993). 'If I were a boy . . .': Constructing knowledge about gender issues in teacher education. *Curriculum Inquiry 23*:367–393.

Enciso, P. (1994). Cultural identity and response to literature: Running lessons from 'Maniac McGee.' *Language Arts, 71*, 524–535.

Entwisle, D.R. (1990). Schools and the adolescent In Feldman, & Elliott, G.R. (Eds.), *At the threshold: The developing adolescent* (pp. 197–224). Cambridge, MA: Harvard University Press.

Ewald, H.R. (1993). Waiting for answerability: Bakhtin and composition studies. *College Composition and Communication 44*:331–348.

Feldman, S. & Elliott, G.R. (1990). Progress and promise of research on adolescence. In Feldman, S. & Elliott, G.R., (Eds.), *At the threshold: The developing adolescent* (pp. 479–505). Cambridge, MA: Harvard University Press.

Ferdman, B.M. (1990). Literacy and cultural identity. *Harvard Educational Review 60*:181–204.

Fine, M. (1994). Working the hyphens: Reinventing self and Other in qualitative research. In N. Denzin & Y. Lincoln (Eds.), *Handbook of qualitative research* (pp. 70–82). Thousand Oaks, CA: Sage.

Fine, M. (1991). *Framing dropouts: Notes of the politics of an urban public high school*. Albany: State University of New York Press.

Fine, M. (1987). Silencing in the public schools. *Language Arts 64*:157–175.

Fine, M. & Zane, N. (1991). Being wrapped too tight: When low-income women drop out of high school. *Women's Studies Quarterly XIX*:77–99.

Finke, L. (1993). Knowledge as bait: Feminism, voice, and the pedagogical unconscious. *College English 55*:7–27.

Finley, M.K. (1992) The educational contest for middle-and-working class women: The reproduction of inequality. In Wrigley, J. (Ed.), *Education and gender equality* (pp. 225–248). London: Falmer Press.

Fish, S. (1980). *Is there a text in this class? The authority of interpretive communities*. Cambridge, MA: Harvard University Press.

Fletcher, R. (1993). *What a writer needs*. Portsmouth, NH: Heinemann.

Flower, L. (1988). The construction of purpose in writing and reading. *College English 50*:528–549.

Freedman, S.W. (1992). Outside-in and inside-out: Peer response groups in two ninth-grade classes. *Research in the Teaching of English 26*:71–107.

Gadsden, V.L. (April 1994). *Private lives in public conversations: The ethics of research across cultural communities*. Paper presented at the Annual Meeting of the American Educational Research Association, New Orleans, LA.

Garbarino, J. & Stott, F.M. (1989). *What children can tell us*. San Francisco, CA: Jossey-Bass.

Gardner, S., Dean, C. & McKaig, D. (1992). Response to difference in the classroom: The politics of knowledge, class, and sexuality. In Wrigley, J. (Ed.), *Education and gender equality* (pp. 131–148). London: Falmer Press.

Gere, A.R., & Abbott, R.D. (1985). Talking about writing: The language of writing groups. *Research in the Teaching of English 19*:362–381.

Gere, A.R., & Stevens, R.S. (1985). The language of writing groups: How oral response shapes revision. In S.W. Freedman (Ed.), *The acquisition of written language* (pp. 85–105). Norwood, NJ: Ablex.

Geertz, C. (1973). *Interpretation of cultures*. New York, NY: Basic Books.

Gilbert, P. (1989). *Writing, schooling, and deconstruction: From voice to text in the classroom*. London: Routledge.

Gilbert, P. & Taylor, S. (1991). *Fashioning the feminine: Girls, popular culture, and schooling*. North Sydney, Australia: Allen & Unwin.

Gilligan, C. (1990). Teaching Shakespeare's sister: Notes from the underground of female adolescence. In Gilligan, C., Lyons, N.P., & Hanmer, T. J., (Eds.), *Making connections: The relational worlds of adolescent girls at Emma Willard School* (pp. 6–29). Cambridge, MA: Harvard University Press.

Gilligan, C. (1982). *In a different voice: Psychological theory and women's development*. Cambridge, MA: Harvard University Press.

Giroux, H. (1983). *Theory and resistance in education: A pedagogy for the opposition*. Boston: Bergin & Garvey.

Goffman, E. (1959). *The presentation of self in everyday life*. Garden City, NY: Doubleday.

Goldstein, L.M. & Conrad, S.M. (1990). Student input and negotiation of meaning in ESL writing conferences. *TESOL Quarterly 24*:443–460.

Graves, D.H. (1983) *Writing: Teachers & children at work*. Portsmouth, NH: Heinemann.

Graves, D.H. & Hansen, J. (1983). The author's chair. *Language Arts 60*:176–183.

Halliday, M.A.K. (1978). *Language as a social semiotic: The social interpretation of language and meaning*. Baltimore, MD: University Park Press.

Harste, J., Short, K., & Burke, C. (Eds.). (1987). *Creating classrooms for authors: The reading-writing connection*. Portsmouth, NH: Heinemann.

Harter, S. (1990). Self and identity development. In Feldman, S. & Elliott, G.R., (Eds.) *At the threshold: The developing adolescent* (pp. 352–387). Cambridge, MA: Harvard University Press.

Hawthorne, R.K. (1992). *Curriculum in the making: Teacher choice and the classroom experience*. New York, NY: Teachers College Press.

Heller, C.E. (1992). *The multiple functions of the tenderloin women writers workshop: Community in the making.* Unpublished doctoral dissertation, University of California, Berkeley.

Herrington, A.J. & Curtis, M. (1990). Basic writing: Moving the voices on the margin to the center. *Harvard Educational Review 60*:489–496.

Hiebert, E.H. (Ed.), (1991). *Literacy for a diverse society.* New York, NY: Teachers College Press.

Hollingsworth, S. (1992). Learning to teach through collaborative conversation: A feminist approach. *American Educational Research Journal 29*:373–404.

Howe, K.R. & K.C. Dougherty (1993). Ethics, institutional review boards, and the changing face of educational research. *Educational Researcher 22*:16–21.

Hudelson, S. (1989). *Write on: children writing in ESL.* Englewood Cliffs, NJ: CAL/ERIC.

Hudelson, S. (1987). The role of native language literacy in the education of language minority children. *Language Arts 64*:827–841.

Humes, A. (1983). Research on the composing process. *Review of Educational Research 53*:201–216.

Israel, B. (1988). *Grown up fast.* New York, NY: Poseidon Press.

Jaffe, A. (1993). Involvement, detachment, and representation of Corsica. In C.B. Brettell (Ed.), *When they read what we write: The politics of ethnography* (pp. 51–66). Westport, CT: Bergin & Garvey.

Kedar-Voivodas, G. (1983). The impact of elementary children's school roles and sex roles on teacher attitudes: An interactional analysis. *Review of Educational Research 53*:415–437.

Kozol, J. (1991). *Savage inequalities.* New York: Crown.

Lane, A.J. (Ed.), (1980). *The Charlotte Perkins Gilman reader.* New York, NY: Pantheon Books.

Langer, J. (1994). A response-based approach to reading literature. *Language Arts, 71,* 203–211.

Langer, J.A. (1991). Literacy and schooling: A sociocognitive perspective. In E.H. Hiebert (Ed.), *Literacy for a diverse society* (pp. 9–27). New York, NY: Teachers College Press.

Langer, J.A. (1985). The child's sense of genre. *Written Communication 2*:157–188.

Lee, P.C. and Gropper, N.B. (1974) Sex-role culture and educational practice. *Harvard Educational Review 44*:369–409.

Lees, S. (1986). *Losing Out: Sexuality and adolescent girls*. London: Hutchinson Education Ltd.

Lensmire, T.J. (1994). *When children write: Critical re-visions of the writing workshop*. New York, NY: Teachers College Press.

Lensmire, T.J. (1993). Following the child, socioanalysis, and threats to the community: Teacher response to children's texts. *Curriculum Inquiry 23*:265–299.

Lewis, M. (1990). Interrupting patriarchy: Politics, resistance, and transformation in the feminist classroom. *Harvard Educational Review 60*:467–488.

Lewis, M. (1988). The construction of femininity embraced in the work of caring for children—Caught between aspirations and reality. *Journal of Educational Thought 22*:259–268.

Lewis, M. & Simon, R.I. (1986). A discourse not intended for her: Learning and teaching within patriarchy. *Harvard Educational Review 56*:457–472.

Lorde, A. (1984). *Sister outsider*. Freedom, CA: Crossing Press.

Luttrell, W. (1992). Working-class women's ways of knowing: Effects of gender, race, and class. In Wrigley, J. (Ed.), *Education and gender equality* (pp. 173–192). London: Falmer Press.

Matthews, A. (1992, November 8). Rage in a tenured position. *The New York Times Magazine*, 46,47,48,72,73,75,83.

McCracken, N.M. (1992). Gender issues and the teaching of writing. In McCracken, N.M. & Appleby, B.C. (Eds.), *Gender issues in the teaching of English*. Portsmouth, NH: Heinemann.

McKenna, T. & Ortiz, F. (1988). *The Broken Web: The educational experience of Hispanic American women*. Berkeley, CA: Floricanto Press.

McGinley, W. & Kamberelis, G. (1992). Transformative functions of children's writing. *Language Arts 69*:330–338.

Michaels, S. (1987). Text and context: A new approach to the study of classroom writing. *Discourse Processes 10*:321–346.

Micucci, D. (1992, May 31). An inspired life: Toni Morrison writes and a generation listens. *The Chicago Tribune*, Section 6, p. 3.

Monahan, B.D. (1984). Revision strategies of basic and competent writers as they write for different audiences. *Research In The Teaching of English 18*:288–303.

Moore, A. (1990). A whole language approach to the teaching of bilingual learners. *Occasional Paper No. 15*. Berkeley, CA: Center for the Study of Writing.

Murray, D. (1968). *A writer teaches writing: A practical method of teaching composition*. Boston: Houghton Mifflin.

Newkirk, T. (1987). The non-narrative writing of young children. *Research in the Teaching of English 21*:121–144.

Noddings, N. (1992). Variability: A pernicious hypothesis. *Review of Educational Research 62*:85–88.

Noddings, N. (1984). *Caring: A feminine approach to ethics and moral education*. Berkeley, CA: University of California Press.

Pappas, C., Kiefer, B., & Levstik, L. (1995). *An integrated language perspective in the elementary school*. White Plains, NY: Longman.

Pappas, C. (1993a). Is narrative 'primary'? Some insights from kindergartners' pretend readings of stories and information books. *Journal of Reading Behavior 25*:97–129.

Pappas, C. (1993b). Understanding texts in contexts: Transforming power relationships in the classroom. *Educational Researcher 22*:25–28.

Pappas, C. (forthcoming). *Learning written genres: A socio-semiotic perspective*. Cresskill, NJ: Hampton Press.

Peshkin, A. (1993). The goodness of qualitative research. *Educational Researcher 22*:24–30.

Peyton, J.K., Staton, J., Richardson, C., & Wolfram. W. (1990). The influence of writing task on ESL students' written production. *Research in the Teaching of English* 24:142–171.

Phinney, J.S. & Rotheram, M. (1987). Ethnic behavior patterns as an aspect of identity. In J.S. Phinney and M. Rotheram (Eds.), *Children's ethnic socialization: Pluralism and development* (pp. 201–218). Newbury, CA: Sage Publications.

Phinney, M.Y. (1991). Literacy and identity: First graders' writing. *Paper presented at the annual conference of the American Educational Research Association*. Chicago, IL.

Powell, R.E. (1991). Teaching the first two R's: Schooled literacy as an ideological construct. *Paper presented at the annual meeting of the National Reading Conference*. Palm Springs, CA.

Prothrow-Stith, D. (1991). *Deadly consequences*. New York, NY: Harper Collins.

Raimes, A. (1985). What unskilled ESL students do as they write: A classroom study of composing. *TESOL Quarterly* 19:229–255.

Raimes, A. (1983). *Techniques in teaching writing*. NY: Oxford University Press.

Reid, B. (1980). *The Indian in the Cupboard*. Garden City, NY: Doubleday.

Reyes, M. (1991). A process approach to literacy instruction for Spanish-speaking students: In search for a best fit. In E.H. Hiebert (Ed.), *Literacy for a Diverse Society* (pp. 157–171). New York, NY: Teachers College Press.

Rogers, A. (1993). Voice, play, and a practice of ordinary courage in girls' and women's lives. *Harvard Educational Review* 63:265–295.

Rogers, A. & Gilligan, C. (1988). Translating girls' voices: Two languages of development. *Harvard Project on the Psychology of Women and the Development of Girls*. Cambridge, MA: Harvard University Graduate School of Education.

Rubin, D.L. & Greene, K. (1992). Gender-typical style in written language. *Research in the Teaching of English* 26:7–40.

Ruiz, R. (1991). The empowerment of language-minority students. In C.E. Sleeter (Ed.), *Empowerment through multicultural education* (pp. 217–227). Albany: State University of New York Press.

Sanford, W. R. (1991). *The World War II soldier at Monte Cassino.* Chicago: Children's Press.

Sassen, G. (1980). Success anxiety in women: A constructivist interpretation of its source and its significance. *Harvard Educational Review 50*:13–24.

Sheehan, E.A. (1993). The student of culture and the ethnography of Irish intellectuals. In C.B. Brettell (Ed.), *When they read what we write: The politics of ethnography* (pp. 1–24). Westport, CT: Bergin & Garvey.

Shuman, A. (1986). *Storytelling rights: The uses of oral and written texts by urban adolescents.* New York: Cambridge University Press.

Singh, B. (1989). What is the gap and how do we bridge it? In Blake, R.W. (Ed.), *Reading, writing, and interpreting literature: Pedagogy, positions, and research.* (pp. 165–183). Schenectady, NY: New York State English Council.

Smith, J.P. (1982). Writing in a remedial reading program: A case study. *Language Arts 59*:245–253.

Sperling, M. & Freedman, S.W. (1987). A good girl writes like a good girl: Written response and clues to the teaching/learning process. *Technical Report No. 3.* Berkeley, CA: The Center for the Study of Writing.

Spencer, M.B. & Dornbusch, S.M. (1990). Challenges in studying minority youth. In Feldman, S. & Elliott, G.R. (Eds.), *At the threshold: The developing adolescent* (pp.123–146). Cambridge, MA: Harvard University Press.

Spradley, J.R. (1980). *Participant observation.* New York, NY: Holt, Reinhart.

Stockard, J. & Wood, J.W. (1984). The myth of female under-achievement: A reexamination of sex differences in academic underachievement. *American Educational Research Journal 21*:825–838.

Sweigart, W. (1991). ~~Classroom talk, knowledge development~~ and writing. *Research in the Teaching of English 25*:469–497.

Talbot, B. (1990). Writing for learning in school: Is it possible? *Language Arts 67*:47–56.

The American Association of University Women Report. (1992). *How schools shortchange girls: A study of major findings on girls and education.* Washington, DC: American Association of University Women Educational Foundation.

Trueba, H.T. (1987). Organizing classroom instruction in specific sociocultural contexts: Teaching Mexican youth to write in English. In S.R. Goldman & H.T. Trueba (Eds.), *Becoming literate in English as a second language* (pp. 235–252). Norwood, NJ: Ablex.

Urzua, C. (1987). "You stopped too soon": Second language children composing and revising. *TESOL Quarterly 21*:279–297.

Walker, C. P. & Elias, D. (1987). Writing conference talk: factors associated with high-and low-rated writing conferences. *Research in the Teaching of English 21*:266–285.

Walmsley, S. (1994). *Children exploring their world.* Portsmouth, NH: Heinemann.

Weiler, K. (1991). Freire and a feminist pedagogy of difference. *Harvard Educational Review 61*:449–475.

Weiler, K. (1988). *Women teaching for change: Gender, class, and power.* New York, NY: Bergin & Garvey.

Weis, L. (1991). Disempowering white working-class females: The role of the high school. In C.E. Sleeter (Ed.), *Empowerment through multicultural education* (pp. 95–121). Albany: State University of New York Press.

Weis, L. & Fine, M. (1993). (Eds.), *Beyond silenced voices: Class, race, and gender in United States schools.* Albany: State University of New York Press.

Weiss, K., Strickland, D., Walmsley, S., & Bronk, G. (1995). Reader response: It's okay to talk in the classroom! *The Language and Literacy Spectrum, 5,* 65–70.

Willinsky, J. (1990). *The new literacy: Redefining reading and writing in the schools.* New York: Routledge.

Wolcott, H.F. (1992). What qualitative research has revealed about education's researchers. *Paper presented at the annual American Educational Research Association conference.* San Francisco, CA.

Wolcott, H.F. (1990). *Writing up qualitative research.* Newbury Park, CA: Sage Publications.

Woolf, V. (1929). *A room of one's own.* New York, NY: Harcourt Brace.

Woods, P. & Hammersley, M. (1993). *Gender and ethnicity in schools: Ethnographic accounts.* London: Routledge.

Wrigley, J. (1992). (Ed.), *Education and gender equality.* London: Falmer Press.

Zamel, V. (1987). Recent research on writing pedagogy. *TESOL Quarterly 21*:697–715.

Zamel, V. (1982). Writing: The process of discovering meaning. *TESOL Quarterly 16*:195–209.

Index